2

# THE BEST TO YOU

## EXTRAORDINARY RECIPES FOR HOME COOKING

# THE BEST TO YOU

## EXTRAORDINARY RECIPES FOR HOME COOKING

by IAN TAYLOR

Order this book online at www.trafford.com/07-2864
or email orders@trafford.com

Most Trafford titles are also available at major online book retailers.


Book design by Ian L. Taylor
Illustrations by Ngaire McKenzie and Elizabeth Knowles.
Cover photography by Andrew Taylor



Note for Librarians: A cataloguing record for this book is available from Library and Archives Canada at www.collectionscanada.ca/amicus/index-e.html

ISBN: 978-1-4251-6265-8

*We at Trafford believe that it is the responsibility of us all, as both individuals and corporations, to make choices that are environmentally and socially sound. You, in turn, are supporting this responsible conduct each time you purchase a Trafford book, or make use of our publishing services. To find out how you are helping, please visit www.trafford.com/responsiblepublishing.html*

*Our mission is to efficiently provide the world's finest, most comprehensive book publishing service, enabling every author to experience success. To find out how to publish your book, your way, and have it available worldwide, visit us online at www.trafford.com/10510*

www.trafford.com

**North America & international**
toll-free: 1 888 232 4444 (USA & Canada)
phone: 250 383 6864 • fax: 250 383 6804 • email: info@trafford.com

**The United Kingdom & Europe**
phone: +44 (0)1865 487 395 • local rate: 0845 230 9601
facsimile: +44 (0)1865 481 507 • email: info.uk@trafford.com

10 9 8 7 6 5 4 3 2 1

# ACKNOWLEDGEMENTS

I would like to acknowledge a few contributors to the evolution and production of this book.

First, there was my Mother, Bernice Taylor, who always had good food cooked for me as a child, and always kept a large collection of good recipes.

Secondly there is Kathryn Knowles who first compiled a number of recipes, hand written in a notebook, that started me out.

I would also like to thank Ngaire McKenzie, my daughter, and Elizabeth Knowles for their contribution of the illustrations here, and Andrew Taylor, my son, for the cover photography.

Diana Knowles was very helpful with some of the older recipes that were not written clearly, and of course contributed a number of the recipes.

I would also like to thank all those who were subjected to the recipes that I developed, particularly Kathryn Knowles and my children, Ngaire, Andrew, and Roger, who took the brunt of my experiments.

Last, but not least, I thank all who have given me encouragement over the years by expressing their appreciation of my earlier attempts at creating a cookbook.

# CONTENTS

# INTRODUCTION

My interest in the world of food came about when I was around six years old. My sister's friend, who's family was from India, offered to make us curry for dinner. I never looked back. The newfound knowledge that there was a world of flavor beyond Britain and Central Europe was a revelation to me. The need to explore never stopped growing. I now search out new flavors from every corner of the globe, being rewarded constantly with new and wonderful things.

The hand written notebook, mentioned in the acknowledgments, lead to the idea of producing a printed book of family recipes. The next stage was to put this book on computer so that it could be updated regularly. At that time, about 1985, few people had home computers. The computer allowed the printing of multiple copies while only typing them in once, unlike using a typewriter. Another advantage of the computer was the ease by which you can create an index. I made copies to be given as gifts to family and friends. The collection grew from there to include the recipes here, and more. After seeing a completely different way of formatting recipes I was inspired to use a modified version of it to retype all of the recipes, also about 1985. People have commented that the combining of the procedures with the ingredients and their amounts is more in line with how people actually cook, while having the ingredients easily scanned, which was not the case with the format that originally inspired me. The new system also does away with the need to read instructions and then go check a separate list for the amounts.

Every Cook Book reflects the taste of its author. This one is no different. Most of the recipes here appeal to a wide range of tastes, as has been demonstrated by family members, some over generations, and many others. One of the reasons for recipes ending up here was the taking of food to pot luck dinners. However, tastes vary widely and the only people these recipes were tested on were from my area of the world. Do not hesitate to modify things as you desire. Many of the recipes here were significantly modified from the originals, for flavor and ease of making. Never, try a recipe on friends without trying it on yourself. You can not always tell if it is going to be a disaster or not. Make the recipe your own by putting your touch to it. Food is meant to be enjoyed, and if you don't enjoy it no one should tell you different. The only judge of what you eat is yourself.

Many people say they don't have enough time to cook fancy meals. The only way anything gets done is that time is set aside for it. Set aside the time to try something new or complicated once a week, or once a month. You will be rewarded with and good food and maybe even praise from family or friends.

This book is intended to appeal to an international audience. However, I do not claim that the recipes are truly authentic to any given cuisine. In this Global World I believe that everyone is borrowing from every other area. In fact the new craze of "Fusion" cooking is nothing new. Tomatoes, as well as chillie peppers, and potatoes, not known outside the Americas before 1492 CE, are used in virtually every cuisine in the world. We borrow the flavors of other parts of the world and adapt them to our own tastes, and the availability of produce, herbs, and spices. In the past the availability of ingredients was regional, often not even national in scope. For example, the designation of a recipe being Chinese is in itself misleading to an extent, since each region of China has its own specialties, largely determined by the climate, the animals available, and what crops could be grown. Now, with the transplanting of crops around the world, and the swiftness of transport, the world has become a global breadbasket, and cuisine itself has become international. Eating habits are probably in greater flux now than in any time in history.

Of course it is best if you use the freshest ingredients possible in any recipe, so acquiring locally grown foods in season is preferred. Fresh and in season foods taste better, which in itself is desirable. The climate in your area will determine how much of the year this is possible. Also, many areas have nutrient deficiencies in their soils. For example most of the soils in British Columbia, where I live, has a relatively serious Selenium deficiency. Selenium is a very important element in a diet. So, in some cases it may be a good idea to vary your food source unless it is known that the grower ensures sufficient levels of all trace elements.

## CONVERSIONS

There have been many different ways of measuring things in different countries in the past. Now we have the metric standard for essentially all countries. The Australian metric tablespoon, which is not standard, is not used in this book. The only situation where measures are relatively critical is in baking, which is not my specialty, but I am assured that as long as the general proportions are kept the same that there should be no problem. Adjustments often need to be made, regardless, due to different flours, humidity, and other factors. UK, US, and Canadian measures can be substituted for the metric standards without much effect on the outcome of most, recipes so long as they are not mixed.

### VOLUME

ABREVIATIONS: Teaspoon=tsp Tablespoon=T Cup=C
Litre=L Millilitre=ml Fluid Ounce=floz Quart=Qt
Pint=pt

| MEASURE | STANDARD METRIC | US | UK/CAN | AUS |
|---|---|---|---|---|
| 1 Liter | 1000 ml | | | |
| 1 Teaspoon | 5 ml | 4.929 ml | 6.16 ml | |
| 1 Dessertspoon | 10 ml | | 12.32 ml (UK only) | |
| 1 Tablespoon | 15 ml | 14.79 ml | 18.48 ml | 20 ml |
| 1 Cup | 250 ml | 236.6 ml | 285 ml | |
| 1 Breakfast Cup | | | 284 ml (UK only) | |
| 1/2 Cup | 125 ml | 118.3 ml | 142.5 ml | |
| 1/3 Cup | 83 ml | 78.7 ml | 95 ml | |
| 1/4 Cup | 62.5 ml | 59.15 ml | 71.25 ml | |
| 1 Fluid Ounce | | 29.57 ml | 28.4 ml | |
| 1 Pint | | 473 ml | 568 ml | |
| 1 Quart | | 946.3 ml | 1.136 L | |

## WEIGHT

Abreviations: Kilogram=kg Pound=lb gram=g Ounce=oz

| | Metric | Imperial/US |
|---|---|---|
| 1 Kilogram | 1000 g | 2.2 Pounds |
| | 453.59 g | 1 Pound |
| | 226.8 g | 1/2 Pound |
| | 113.4 g | 1/4 Pound |
| | 28.35 g | 1 Ounce |

## TEMPERATURE

| CELCIUS | FAHRENHEIT | GASMARK (Regulo) |
|---|---|---|
| 120 | 250 | 1/2 |
| 135 | 275 | 1 |
| 150 | 300 | 2 |
| 165 | 325 | 3 |
| 180 | 350 | 4 |
| 190 | 375 | 5 |
| 205 | 400 | 6 |
| 220 | 425 | 7 |
| 230 | 450 | 8 |
| 245 | 475 | 9 |

# LENGTH

| METRIC | IMPERIAL |
|---|---|
| 3 mm | 1/8 inch |
| 6 mm | 1/4 inch |
| 13 mm | 1/2 inch |
| 2.5 cm | 1 inch |
| 5 cm | 2 inches |
| 7.6 cm | 3 inches |
| 10 cm | 4 inches |
| 13 cm | 5 inches |
| 15 cm | 6 inches |
| 18 cm | 7 inches |
| 20 cm | 8 inches |
| 23 cm | 9 inches |
| 25 cm | 10 inches |
| 28 cm | 11 inches |
| 30 cm | 12 inches |

# INGREDIENTS

Many of the ingredients here will seem, to some, to be exotic and unusual However, even here on Vancouver Island, off the west coast of Canada all the ingredients in this book are available. They can be found at everyday grocery stores or in specialized Indian, Chinese, Middle Eastern, or Japanese grocers.

If you can not find something for a recipe try something similar, or, if it does not seem critical, leave it out. I have often done this and then later, after finding the missing ingredient, done the recipe again with the correct item, discovering that the difference is negligible. It has even been the case that a recipe has turned out better with the "wrong" ingredient. On the other hand, I have followed recipes to the letter which ended in disaster, at least to my taste. Hopefully this is not the case with the recipes here. If even with this list you are still having problems the Internet can be a wonderful place.

AUBERGINE: See eggplant

BAMBOO SHOOTS: The young shoots of a large Asian bamboo plant.

BERRY SUGAR: Synonyms - superfine sugar, castor sugar.

BLACK BEAN SAUCE: A Chinese sauce made with fermented black beans, found in thick or thin varieties.

BLACK MUSHROOM: See dried black mushrooms

BLACK VINEGAR: A type of Chinese rice vinegar.

BUTTON MUSHROOM: Synonym - field mushroom. A white to light brown mushroom widely used fresh in western cooking.

CAPSICUM PEPPER: Includes all types of mild to hot chilli types and sweet bell peppers.

CARDAMOM: Usually found as pods which contain a number of seeds. They are found in a variety of colors from green to dark brown. The green version is the most used

CAYENNE PEPPER: (See CAUTION under CHILLIES.): Synonyms - red pepper. A type of chilli pepper used extensively fresh and dried in India and around the world.

CHILI POWDER: Distinguished from chillies and red pepper powder in that this is a mixture of spices.

CHILLIES: Spicy members of the capsicum pepper family. CAUTION: When handling fresh or dried chillies either use rubber gloves or rinse hands thoroughly afterwards and avoid touching any sensitive areas, such as the eyes. The burning sensation does no permanent harm but it can be very uncomfortable. There are at least hundreds of varieties, from very small to quite large. They also vary widely in strength, even within the same type. There seems to be no hard and fast rule to the spelling of this ingredient, so the spelling I have chosen follows the Aztec pronunciation, as recorded in the Oxford Dictionary. This also distinguishes the name from the popular stew like dish called chili, and chili powder, which is a mixture of dried chillies and other spices.

CHILLI GARLIC SAUCE: A sauce usually made up of chillies, garlic, and vinegar.

CHILLI OIL: The result of chillies being, heated in oil and the oil strained. Sometimes other flavorings such as ginger or Sichuan peppercorns are added, during the process.

CHINESE SAUSAGE: Used largely as a flavoring. Must be cooked.

CHINESE WHITE RADISH: Synonyms – Chinese turnip, daikon radish. A large long spicy radish somewhat the same size and shape of a carrot.

CHORIZO SAUSAGE: A Spanish spicy cured sausage.

CILANTRO: See coriander leaf.

CONFECTIONERS' SUGAR: See Icing Sugar.

CORIANDER LEAF: Synonyms - Cilantro, Chinese parsley, Mexican parsley, green coriander. The fresh leaf of the coriander plant. Stems and roots are used as well.

CORIANDER POWDER: Ground coriander seed.

CORIANDER SEED: The small round seed of the coriander plant found whole, and as a powder.

CORN: Synonyms, as used in this book - maize, Indian(American) corn, sweet corn

CORN STARCH: Starch separated from corn (maize). You can substitute tapioca starch or arrowroot.

CUMIN: Seeds are black or brown, the black being the most used in India. Can be found as seeds or powder.

CURRY LEAF: The leaf of a shrub, smaller than, but somewhat the same shape as, a Bay leaf. Usually found dried whole where you would get Indian spices.

CURRY POWDER: An Indian spice mixture which can vary greatly, depending on the region it is from. Most Western cooks recommend a version of Madras curry powder, but keep in mind that that only represents the Madras area of India, which is why I use curry powder sparingly in Indian recipes, preferring to use individual spices.

DRIED BLACK MUSHROOMS: A dried version of Shiitake mushroom. Used widely in Chinese cooking. Should be soaked about 25 minutes to soften and squeezed to remove some of the moisture before use. Stems are discarded, being very tough.

EGGPLANT: Synonym - Aubergine.

FENUGREEK: An irregular yellow to brown seed.

FERMENTED BLACK BEANS: Synonyms - salted black beans, preserved black beans, Chinese black beans. These are salted and fermented soy beans. Sometimes Ginger is included in the process. They can be used as is, or rinsed to reduce the saltiness of a dish.

FISH SAUCE: A sauce made of fermented fish used extensively in South East Asia. Similar to anchovies in use, and to the ancient garum sauce used extensively by the Romans.

FIVE SPICE POWDER: Synonym - five flavor, or five fragrances. A Chinese spice mixture.

GARAM MASALA: An Indian spice mixture.

GARBANZO BEANS: Synonym - chick peas, ceci beans.

GARLIC: Fresh garlic is usually found as a whole bulb, which is sometimes referred to as a head, consisting of a number of bulblets. These bulblets are usually called cloves or toes.

GHEE: Clarified butter.

GLUTINOUS RICE: Synonyms - sticky rice, sweet rice.

GREEN ONIONS: See Scallion

HAZEL NUT: Synonym - Filbert

HOISIN SAUCE: A Chinese sauce, to be found in most grocers.

HOMINY CORN (maize): Synonym - Samp. Corn kernels with the outer skin removed. Usually found canned.

HOT BEAN PASTE: A paste made of soy beans and chillies.

ICING SUGAR: Synonyms - confectioners' sugar, superfine sugar. A finely powdered sugar.

KETCHUP: Synonyms - catsup, catchup. Usually refers to a type of tomato sauce, as it does here, but there is also a form of mushroom ketchup.

LEMON GRASS: Synonym - citronella (Europe). A grass which gives the scent and flavor of lemon without the acidity.

LOTUS LEAF: The round leaf of an Asian aquatic plant measuring about 60 cm (two feet) across. It has a tea like flavor. Usually found dried in bundles.

MARJORUM: Mild species of Origanum. Related to oregano but much milder in flavor.

MUSTARD SEED: Found as yellow, black, and brown. Yellow is used mostly in the West. Black is most used in India. Brown is hotter than the others.

OREGANO: Origanum Vulgara, or wild oregano. Varies widely in it's strength. Wild Greek oregano is what is used in the recipes here. It is quite spicy. Occasionally marjoram is named oregano, which is not entirely false, being a species of Oreganum as well, but it is much weaker in flavor.

PABLANO CHILLI: A mild to hot, medium large dark green bell shaped chilli pepper, with good flavor.

PAPRIKA: A type of capiscum pepper, particularly from Hungary, usually found ground to a powder. The powder can vary from sweet to quite hot.

PRAWNS: Synonym – jumbo shrimp.

RED PEPPER: Synonyms - cayenne pepper. Dried hot red chilli peppers. Found whole, flaked, and powdered, everywhere. For most of the recipes here you can use as little or as much as you like. Red pepper is used to spice things up, not to add flavor. Sometimes powdered it is called pure chili powder.

REFRIED BEANS: Fried mashed beans used in Mexican cooking. Usually found canned.

SALTED BLACK BEANS: See fermented black beans

SCALLION: Synonyms - green onions, spring onions. A mild small onion of which the bulb and leaves are used.

SESAME OIL: The oil extracted from sesame seeds. Used mostly as a flavoring near the end of cooking and for salads, much like olive oil is used.

SICHUAN PEPPERCORNS: Synonyms - anise pepper, brown pepper, flower pepper, Chinese aromatic pepper, Chinese pepper, Szechuan (the old spelling of Sichuan) peppercorns. A small berry from a type of Asian ash tree. Substitutes – Japanese fagara pepper, which is from a similar tree.

SNOW PEAS: A Chinese pod pea which can be eaten pod and all. Can substitute mange tout or sugar pea.

STAR ANISE: Synonyms - anise, whole anise, Chinese anise. A star shaped seed pod used widely in China as a spice.

STRAW MUSHROOM: Generally only available canned.

SUET: A crumbly beef fat.

SZECHUAN PEPPERCORNS: See Sichuan peppercorns

TAHINI: Synonym - Tahina. Sesame seed paste.

TOFU: Synonyms - Bean curd, toufu. Made from yellow soy beans.

TURMERIC: Usually used as a powder, mostly for the yellow color.

WATER CHESTNUTS: Not a chestnut. They are a crunchy root vegetable used primarily for their texture.

WILD RICE: A relative to the more common rice types. It is much denser and takes at least half again longer to cook than most rice.

ZEST: The grated outer rind of an orange, a lemon, or a lime.

ZUCCHINI: Synonym - courgette

# APPETIZERS AND DIPS

## ONION AND SPINACH PAKORA

INTO A BOWL PUT

1 1/2 C besan (gram) flour (chickpea flour), or all purpose flour

RUB IN

1 T vegetable oil

ADD

2 T cilantro, (fresh coriander leaves), chopped
1 tsp garam masala
1 tsp red pepperowder
1 tsp cumin powder
1 tsp dried oregano
1 fresh green chilli, chopped finely
1 tsp salt

MIX AND ADD

warm water, enough to form a thick batter

ADD, MIXING IN

1 medium onion, halved and sliced thinly
50 g (2 oz) spinach, chopped

FRY, ON HIGH, 2 OR 3 TABLESPOONS AT A TIME, IN

1.3 cm (1/2 inch) vegetable oil

BEING CAREFUL NOT TO LET THE OIL GET TOO COOL, OR TOO HOT.

## SPRING ROLLS

(makes about 15)

INTO A BOWL PUT

500 g (1 lb) chicken, or pork, cooked and shredded

AND RESERVE

INTO A LARGE POT PUT

3 T vegetable oil

1 tsp sesame oil

HEAT AND ADD

5 dried black mushrooms, soaked 25 minutes and excess water squeezed out, and diced, discard stems.

STIR 30 SECONDS AND ADD

1/2 C bamboo shoots, shredded

2 C bean sprouts

STIR FRY 2 MINUTES AND ADD

3 T soy sauce

STIR AND ADD A MIXTURE OF

2 tsp cornstarch, or tapioca starch

2 T water

STIR FRY UNTIL VEGETABLES ARE GLAZED AND ADD

1 T sesame oil

STIR A BIT AND POUR OVER CHICKEN. MIX WELL AND LET COOL.

WRAP CHICKEN MIXTURE IN

Egg roll skins

SEALING EDGES WITH A MIXTURE OF

1 T cornstarch

2 T water

1 egg yolk

DEEP FRY AT 190 C (375 F) UNTIL GOLDEN BROWN.

LET COOL SLIGHTLY BEFORE EATING.

These samosas are simply scrumptious. The spices added to the wrapping gives an extra layer of flavor.

## SAMOSAS

TO MAKE THE WRAPPERS SIFT INTO A BOWL

2 C maida, or all purpose flour
1 tsp garam masala
1 tsp salt
1/2 tsp turmeric powder
1/2 tsp black pepper, ground
1/4 tsp red pepper powder

ADD

2 T vegetable oil
Water, enough to make a very thick dough.

WRAP IN A CLOTH AND SET ASIDE FOR 20 MINUTES.

TO MAKE THE FILLING FRY UNTIL COLORED

250 g (1/2 lb) lean ground beef or lamb

ADD

3/4 C onion, chopped finely
3 tsp garlic, chopped finely
2 tsp fresh ginger, grated

FRY 2 MINUTES AND ADD

2 tsp garam masala
1/2 tsp turmeric powder
1/2 tsp red pepper powder

STIR AND ADD

1 T lemon juice
1/2 tsp salt

ADD

1 T cilantro, (fresh coriander leaf), or parsley, chopped
3/4 C peas

MIX THOROUGHLY, REMOVE FROM HEAT, AND COOL. FORM DOUGH INTO 1 INCH BALLS AND ROLL THINLY INTO 10 TO 13 cm (4 to 5 inch) ROUNDS. CUT THE ROUNDS IN HALF. WET HALF OF THE WRAPPER EDGE AND PLACE 1 TABLESPOON OF FILLING ON THE WRAPPER. FOLD

WRAPPER OVER, AND PRESS EDGES TOGETHER WELL. DEEP FRY UNTIL GOLDEN BROWN. OTHER FILLINGS MAY BE SUBSTITUTED. MAIDA FLOUR WILL MAKE SAMOSAS MUCH MORE CRISP.

## KOREAN SESAME BEEF SLICES

SLICE

1 kg (2 lb) lean beef into 5cm x 3 mm (2x1/8 inch) pieces

PLACE IN A BOWL AND ADD A MIXTURE OF

2 T sesame seeds, toasted and ground
4 scallions, cut in 5 cm (2 inch) lengths
4 garlic cloves, chopped finely
1/3 C soy sauce
2 T sugar
2 T sesame oil
2 T dry sherry, or rice wine
1 tsp fresh ginger, grated
1 tsp black pepper, ground

LET THE MEAT MARINATE FOR 2 HOURS.

MAKE A SAUCE OF

3 T soy sauce
2 tsp sesame oil
1 tsp hot bean paste, or 1/2 tsp red pepper powder
2 T water
2 T sherry or rice wine
2 tsp sesame seeds, toasted and ground
1 scallion, chopped finely
1 tsp chilli garlic sauce
2 garlic cloves, chopped finely
2 tsp sugar

MIX AND LET STAND TO BLEND THE FLAVORS.
GRILL MEAT SLICES AND SERVE WITH THE SAUCE.

These have always been a hit with family and friends.

## SESAME CHICKEN WINGS

(220 C (425 F) - 30 minutes)

IN A LARGE BOWL COMBINE

1/3 C soy sauce
2 T honey
2 T cider vinegar
1 T fresh ginger, grated
1 T sesame oil
2 garlic cloves, chopped finely
1/4 tsp red pepper powder

ADD, STIRRING TO COAT

1.5 kg (3 lb) chicken wings, cut in sections

MARINATE AT ROOM TEMPERATURE FOR 2 HOURS, OR REFRIGERATE OVER NIGHT.

STIR, PUT ON RACKS ON A BAKING PAN, AND SPRINKLE WITH

3 T sesame seeds

BAKE AS ABOVE.

TO REHEAT NEXT DAY BAKE AT 180 C (350 F) FOR 10 TO 15 MINUTES. GREAT COLD TOO.

## JAPANESE CHICKEN WINGS

(180 C (350 F) 30 minutes)

DIP, ONE PIECE AT A TIME
1.5 kg (3 lb) chicken wings, cut in sections
IN
1 egg, beaten
THEN IN
All purpose flour
BROWN IN A FRYING PAN UNTIL CRISP AND TRANSFER THEM TO A BAKING DISH.
TO A SMALL POT ADD
3 T soy sauce
3 T water
1 C sugar
1/2 C vinegar
1/2 tsp salt
1 1/2 T corn starch
MIX WELL AND BRING TO A BOIL.
STIR UNTIL THICKENED AND POUR OVER WINGS.
BAKE AS ABOVE.

## HONEY FIVE SPICE WINGS

IN A BOWL COMBINE

1/3 C soy sauce
1 T honey
2 T dry sherry, or wine
2 T peanut oil, or vegetable oil
2 tsp sesame oil
3 garlic cloves, chopped finely
2 tsp fresh ginger, grated
1/2 tsp five spice powder
1 T cilantro (fresh coriander leaves), chopped

ADD

8 chicken pieces

MIX TOGETHER AND MARINATE CHICKEN IN THE FRIDGE 2 HOURS OR MORE.
GRILL UNTIL DONE.

## MEXICAN BROILED GARLIC PRAWNS

IN A SMALL SAUCEPAN MELT

5 T butter

AND ADD

3 garlic cloves, chopped finely
1 tsp red pepper powder
1 T lime, or lemon juice

SIMMER 1 MINUTE.
ONTO SKEWERS PUT

500 g (1 lb) prawns (jumbo shrimp)

BROIL, WHILE BASTING WITH SAUCE, TURNING ONCE, UNTIL JUST PINK, ABOUT 3 MINUTES.

## DEEP FRIED BACON WRAPPED OYSTERS

IN A BOWL COMBINE
1 tsp fresh ginger, grated
2 T soy sauce
2 T sherry, or wine
ADD
12 oysters
AND LET STAND 15 MINUTES, TURNING OCCASIONALLY.
DRAIN AND DISCARD MARINADE.
CRUSH, ALMOST TO A POWDER
1 C mixed nuts
COAT EACH OYSTER WITH THE CRUSHED NUTS.
TOP WITH SOME OF
3 T smoked ham, slivered
AND A PIECE OF
2 scallion stalks, cut in 1.3 cm (1/2 inch) sections
WRAP WITH A PIECE OF
3 bacon strips, cut in 4 pieces
FOR BATTER BLEND
1 egg, lightly beaten
1/2 C all purpose flour
Salt
Black pepper, ground
DIP OYSTERS IN A BATTER AND DEEP FRY UNTIL GOLDEN AND CRISP

The results here are surprising and wonderful.

## CHILLI RAJAS

UNDER A BROILER ROAST UNTIL SKIN SEPARATES SOMEWHAT, TURNING FOR AN EVEN EFFECT.

4 fresh pablano, or pasilla chillies

PUT THEM IN A PLASTIC BAG FOR 5 OR 10 MINUTES.
REMOVE AND PEEL AS WELL AS YOU CAN.
DE-SEED THE CHILLIES, CUT IN 1.3 cm (1/2 inch) STRIPS, AND SET ASIDE.
IN A FRYING PAN HEAT

1 1/2 T olive oil

ADD

1 medium onion, sliced 6 mm (1/4 inch) thick

AND FRY UNTIL BROWN.
ADD THE CHILLI STRIPS AND

2 garlic cloves, chopped
1/2 tsp dried oregano
1/2 tsp dried basil
1/2 tsp dried thyme

FRY, MIXING, UNTIL HEATED WELL AND ADD

2/3 C milk
1/4 tsp salt

COOK ON MEDIUM, STIRRING, UNTIL LIQUID IS REDUCED AND COATS THE VEGETABLES LIKE A GLAZE.

## HUMOUS

PUT THE FOLLOWING IN A FOOD PROCESSOR AND BLEND.

500 ml (19 oz) can garbanzo beans (chickpeas), drained
3 T lemon juice
1 T tahini
1 T fresh parsley, chopped finely
1/2 tsp salt
dash black pepper, ground
1 garlic clove, crushed

## CRAB DIP

COMBINE AND MIX WELL

250 g (8 oz) cream cheese, softened
2 T mayonnaise
3/4 tsp Worcestershire sauce
1/4 tsp salt
1 T onion, chopped finely
90 g (3 oz) crab meat
1 T lemon juice

# SOUPS

This soup is easy and popular.

## HAMBURGER SOUP

BOIL UNTIL TENDER
250 g (1/2 lb) dry white beans
IN A LARGE POT BROWN
125 g (1/4 lb) ground beef
ADD
10 C water, or half water and half beef broth
2 C tomato juice
1 kg (2 lb) tomatoes
4 beef bouillon cubes
3/4 C rice ,uncooked, or shredded potato
1 1/2 C celery, finely chopped
1 1/2 C onion, finely chopped
1 1/2 C carrots, shredded
1 tsp salt
2 T soy sauce
1/4 tsp dried marjoram, or oregano
1/4 tsp dried thyme
Black pepper, ground
ADD THE BEANS, BRING TO A BOIL, AND SIMMER 2 HOURS. THIS IS A BASIC SOUP, SO YOU CAN ADD ANY VEGETABLES YOU LIKE.

## AFRICAN PEANUT BUTTER MEAT SOUP

INTO A LARGE POT PUT

1.5 kg (3 lb) chicken, or other meat, cubed
1 medium onion, chopped
1 tsp salt
1 tsp black pepper, ground
1 tsp curry powder
1 tsp red pepper powder
1/2 C water

COOK OVER MEDIUM HEAT FOR 15 MINUTES, STIRRING ONCE OR TWICE. REMOVE THE CHICKEN FROM THE POT AND RESERVE.

TO THE POT ADD

1 C smooth peanut butter
8 C warm water

STIR UNTIL SMOOTH AND RETURN THE CHICKEN MIXTURE. BRING TO A BOIL. BOIL FOR 30 MINUTES.

ADD

2 T tomato paste

LOWER HEAT, SIMMER UNTIL SOUP THICKENS, AND OIL BEGINS TO FORM ON TOP, ABOUT 1 1/2 HOURS.

## DOMINICAN CHICKEN SOUP

MARINATE FOR 1 HOUR OR MORE
1.5 kg (3 lb) chicken, skinned and cut up
IN
1/4 C seville (bitter) orange juice, or (3 T orange and 1 T lemon)
MIX OCCASIONALLY. AFTER MARINATING DRAIN AND DISCARD JUICE.
PUT THE CHICKEN IN A LARGE POT WITH
chicken giblets (optional)
250 g (1/2 lb) calabaza squash, or other firm squash, cubed
6 C chicken stock
1 bay leaf
2 allspice berries
2 fresh red chillies, chopped finely
1 T cilantro (fresh coriander leaves) chopped
1 T fresh parsley, chopped
1 large onion, chopped
3 garlic cloves, chopped finely
BRING TO A BOIL, LOWER HEAT, AND SIMMER 25 MINUTES.
ADD
500 g (1 lb) potatoes, peeled and sliced
250 g (1/2 lb) carrots, peeled and sliced
500 g (1 lb) tomatoes, chopped
1 tsp salt
SIMMER UNTIL THE VEGETABLES ARE TENDER AND ADD
2 T vinegar
MIX AND SERVE.

## CHICKEN WITH PRAWNS AND COCONUT SOUP

INTO A POT PUT

2 C chicken stock, or water

1 tsp salt

2 chicken breasts

BRING TO A BOIL, LOWER HEAT, AND SIMMER FOR 30 MINUTES.

ADD

1/2 C straw mushrooms, or button mushrooms

2 sprigs lemongrass, or 2 tsp lemon juice

4 cafir lime leaves (optional)

2 dry red pepper, crushed

2 T fish sauce (optional)

1 tsp fresh ginger, grated

1 can coconut milk

BRING TO A BOIL, REDUCE HEAT, AND SIMMER 20 MINUTES.

ADD

8 prawns (jumbo shrimp)

2 T lime juice

2 T cilantro (fresh coriander leaves), chopped

COOK 5 MINUTES AND SERVE.

# MULLIGATAWNY SOUP

CUT UP AND SKIN
1 stewing chicken
PUT THE CHICKEN IN A LARGE POT WITH
6 onions, sliced
3 garlic cloves, chopped
3 L (3 quarts) water
3 slices fresh ginger 3 mm (1/8 inch) thick
2 pieces cinnamon, 5 cm (2 inches) long
6 tomatoes, chopped
1 bay leaf
1/2 tsp coriander powder
1 tsp salt
BRING TO A BOIL AND LOWER HEAT TO SIMMER UNTIL THE CHICKEN IS TENDER. STRAIN OFF THE STOCK AND RESERVE THE BOTH.
GRIND THE FOLLOWING TO A POWDER.
10 dried red chillies, crushed, or to taste
1 T coriander powder
1 1/2 tsp cumin powder
1 1/2 tsp turmeric powder
1 T fresh ginger, grated,
1/2 tsp black pepper, ground
AND PUT IT IN A MEDIUM POT WITH
1 1/2 C coconut milk
ADD 5 CUPS OF THE STOCK TO THE POT AND STIR INTO THE COCONUT MIXTURE. SIMMER UNTIL IT THICKENS A LITTLE.
HEAT A SAUCEPAN AND ADD
1 T ghee, or vegetable oil
1 onion, sliced
AND FRY UNTIL GOLDEN.
ADD THE ONION TO THE SOUP ABOUT 5 MINUTES BEFORE SERVING. SERVE WITH RICE, SLICES OF LIME, AND THE CHICKEN CUT IN SMALL PIECES.

# POZOLE (Chicken Pork Soup)

IN A LARGE POT COMBINE

6 C chicken stock
3 pigs feet, split, or pork-hocks
1 stewing chicken, cut up
1 head garlic, about 10 cloves, peeled and chopped
1 large onion, sliced
water, enough to cover

BRING TO A BOIL, LOWER HEAT, AND SIMMER 2 HOURS. SKIM FAT FROM SURFACE AND ADD

500 g (1 lb) boneless pork, cut in 2.5 cm (1 inch) cubes

SIMMER ANOTHER HOUR AND SKIM FAT IF NECESSARY. REMOVE PIGS FEET OR HOCKS, DEBONE, CUT IN 1 INCH PIECES AND RETURN TO SOUP.

ADD

2 540 ml (19 oz) Cans hominy corn, drained
2 tsp salt
1 tsp black pepper, ground
1 pinch baking soda

BRING BACK TO A BOIL, LOWER HEAT, AND SIMMER 1/2 HOUR. SERVE WITH THE FOLLOWING GARNISHES SEPARATE.

1 C sliced radishes
1 C shredded lettuce
1/2 C onions chopped
1 T dried oregano
1 T dried red chillies crumbled
2 limes, cut in wedges
2 T fresh or canned chillies, chopped
1 C salsa
1/2 C monterey jack cheese, grated
1 C cilantro (fresh coriander leaves), chopped

This is a very popular Chinese soup.

## HOT AND SOUR SOUP

IN A LARGE POT BRING TO A BOIL
8 C chicken stock, or water
ADD
125 g (1/4 lb) lean pork, shredded
2 dried black mushrooms, soaked 15 minutes, water squeezed out,and shredded, (discard stems)
3 fresh ginger slices, 3 mm (1/8 inch) thick
2 wood ear mushrooms, soaked and shredded (optional)
COOK 2 TO 3 MINUTES AND DISCARD THE GINGER.
ADD
1/2 square firm tofu, shredded 6 mm x6 mm x5 cm (1/4x1/4x2 inch) pieces
1/4 C bamboo shoots, shredded
2 T button mushrooms, sliced
1 slice ham, shredded
1/2 C vinegar
1 tsp black pepper, ground
3/4 tsp salt
1 tsp sesame oil
3/4 tsp sugar
1 T soy sauce
1 tsp chilli oil, or 1/2 tsp red pepper powder
REDUCE HEAT AND SIMMER 2 MINUTES.
ADD, MIXING IN, A MIXTURE OF
3 T water
4 T corn starch
COOK UNTIL THICKENED AND CLEAR.
REMOVE FROM HEAT AND SLOWLY STIR IN
2 eggs, lightly beaten
SERVE IMMEDIATELY. CAN BE REHEATED BUT NOT AS GOOD.

I have placed this soup under Lamb because the original version was similar. However, with experimentation I found that it is equally good with any meat, or poultry. It is a very versatile combination. Besides, the children loved it.

## LAMB SOUP

TO A LARGE POT ADD

2 T vegetable oil

HEAT AND ADD

1 medium onion, chopped finely
8 garlic cloves, chopped
1 tsp red pepper powder

FRY UNTIL GOLDEN BROWN

ADD

6 C lamb broth, or water
5 C lamb, cooked and cut in 13 mm (1/2 inch) cubes
1 tsp salt
1 tsp black pepper, ground
1 tsp dried basil
1 tsp dried oregano

BRING TO A BOIL AND LOWER HEAT. SIMMER AT LEAST 30 MINUTES. ABOUT 40 MINUTES BEFORE SERVING ADD

6 carrots, or other vegetables, sliced
6 potatoes, cubed

SIMMER UNTIL THE CARROTS AND POTATOES ARE TENDER AND SERVE.

This has been a staple since I was a child.

## CLAM CHOWDER

IN A LARGE POT HEAT
1 T vegetable oil
ADD
1 onion, chopped
1/2 C lean bacon, chopped
FRY UNTIL THE ONION IS TRANSPARENT AND ADD
4 potatoes, peeled and diced
3 carrots, peeled and diced
juice from 2 400 ml (14oz) cans of clams
water to cover
BRING TO A BOIL, LOWER HEAT AND SIMMER 20 MINUTES.
ADD
1 C corn kernels
clams, from the above cans
BRING TO A BOIL, LOWER HEAT, AND SIMMER 20 MINUTES.
ADD A MIXTURE OF
2 T corn starch
1 C milk
BRING TO A BOIL, STIR CONSTANTLY UNTIL THICK.
REDUCE HEAT AND COOK UNTIL VEGETABLES ARE TENDER.

## GHANA FISHERMAN'S SOUP

INTO A LARGE POT PUT

5 C water

AND ADD

1 tsp salt

1 small onion, grated

2 tomatoes, whole

1 tsp red pepper powder

BOIL 15 MINUTES AND THEN REDUCE HEAT TO MEDIUM. REMOVE THE TOMATOES, MASH THEM AND STRAIN PULP INTO THE SOUP. BRING THE SOUP TO A BOIL AGAIN AND ADD

1 kg (2 lb) firm white fish, cut in bite size pieces

SIMMER ANOTHER 25 MINUTES AND ADD

125 g (1/4 lb) shrimp, (optional)

SIMMER 5 MINUTES AND SERVE.

This recipe requires care, particularly the making of the croutons, but worth it when done well.

## GARLIC SOUP WITH CROUTONS

IN A LARGE POT HEAT
1/3 C olive oil
1/4 C butter, or margarine
ADD
16 garlic cloves, peeled
FRY UNTIL GOLDEN ON THE OUTSIDE. REMOVE GARLIC, MASH, AND RESERVE.
ADD THE FOLLOWING TO THE OIL
1/2 tsp sweet paprika powder
1/4 tsp red pepper powder
1 tsp salt
1/4 tsp black pepper, ground
STIR A FEW SECONDS. ENSURE THE OIL IS HOT ENOUGH BY TESTING WITH A PIECE OF BREAD AND ADD
3 C bread, cut in 1.3 cm (1/2 inch) cubes
FRY UNTIL GOLDEN BROWN, BEING CAREFUL TO NOT BURN THEM. REMOVE, SET ON PAPER TOWELS TO DRAIN, AND RESERVE.
TO THE POT ADD
olive oil, if needed, to total 3 tablespoons
1/4 tsp sweet paprika powder
1/4 tsp red pepper powder
1/2 tsp salt
STIR A FEW TIMES AND ADD
6 C chicken stock, or water
BRING TO A BOIL AND ADD MASHED GARLIC. REDUCE HEAT AND SIMMER 30 MINUTES. SERVE WITH CROUTONS, PLACING SOME IN EACH BOWL.

## PUMPKIN BISQUE

IN A POT HEAT

1 T vegetable oil

1 T butter

ADD

1 large onion, chopped

FRY UNTIL TRANSLUCENT AND ADD

1 1/2 tsp dried chillies, crushed

5 garlic cloves, chopped

COOK FOR 3 MINUTES AND ADD

750 g (1 1/2 lb) pumpkin, diced, or a 450 ml (16 oz) can of pumpkin

4 C chicken stock

1/2 tsp black pepper, ground

1/4 tsp allspice, grated

1/2 tsp sugar

1/4 C dry sherry, or wine

SIMMER 30 MINUTES AND PROCESS IN FOOD PROCESSOR UNTIL SMOOTH.

RETURN TO THE POT AND ADD

1 C milk ,or light cream

BRING TO A SIMMER AND SERVE SPRINKLED WITH

Nutmeg, grated

This is a little something developed on the spur of the moment. At the time I grew broccoli, globe artichokes, and oregano in the back yard and chillies in my greenhouse. This combination came about.

## BROCCOLI SOUP a la MAISON

INTO A POT PUT

4 C chicken stock
3 C broccoli, cut into 2.5 cm (1 inch) pieces
1 tsp salt
2 fresh green chilli peppers, chopped finely
1 tsp black pepper
3 fresh artichoke hearts, chopped
1 medium onion, chopped
1 tsp dried oregano

BRING TO A BOIL, LOWER HEAT, AND SIMMER 30 TO 40 MINUTES.

This soup was adopted to use my bumper crop of tomatoes.

## TOMATO SOUP

IN A POT HEAT

2 T olive oil

ADD

2 onions, chopped

FRY UNTIL TRANSLUCENT AND ADD

10 garlic cloves, sliced
2 celery stalks, chopped
4 L (4 Quarts) tomatoes, peeled and chopped
1 tsp sugar
1 tsp dried basil
1 tsp dried oregano
1 tsp salt
1/2 tsp black pepper, ground
1 T fresh parsley, chopped finely

SIMMER 2 HOURS ON LOW.

# PISTOU SOUP

PLACE IN A POT AND BRING TO A BOIL
3 C stock, or water
ADD
3/4 C navy beans, soaked
AND BOIL 2 MINUTES. LOWER HEAT AND COOK UNTIL TENDER. DRAIN AND RESERVE. SAVE LIQUID.

PISTO
IN A BOWL MASH TOGETHER
2 garlic cloves, chopped finely
5 T dried basil
ADD
2 T tomato paste
1/2 C parmesan cheese
BEAT IN
6 T olive oil
AND RESERVE.
IN A HEAVY POT HEAT
4 T olive oil
1 C onion, diced
1 1/2 C tomatoes, peeled and chopped
3 L (3 quarts) water
1 1/2 C carrots, diced
1 1/2 C potatoes, diced
1 C leeks, chopped
1/2 C celery leaves, chopped
1 1/2 C green beans
1 1/2 C zucchini, diced
COOK FOR 15 MINUTES AND ADD THE RESERVED NAVY BEANS, STOCK, AND PISTOU. BRING TO A BOIL AND REMOVE FROM HEAT AND SPRINKLE THE SOUP WITH
1 1/2 C parmesan cheese

The soup here was originally intended for the use of my often large chilli crop. It is very spicy, so beware.

## CHILLI SOUP

IN A POT HEAT

2 T vegetable oil

ADD AND FRY UNTIL TRANSLUCENT

1 large onion, chopped finely

ADD

1 C fresh green and red chillies, deseeded and chopped
6 garlic cloves, chopped
1 piece fresh ginger, about 3 cm (1 inch) long, grated

COOK UNTIL SOFTENED AND ADD

1 tsp mustard seeds
1/2 tsp allspice, grated
1 tsp dry mustard powder

MIX THOROUGHLY AND ADD

750 g (1 1/2 lb) tomatoes, chopped
1 tsp salt
3 C water

BRING TO A BOIL, LOWER HEAT AND SIMMER 45 MINUTES. FOR A CREAMED SOUP PURE AFTER COOKING AND SIMMER 20 MINUTES.

# SALADS

This Indonesian recipe is a bit complicated, but is a hit at pot luck dinners.

## GADO GADO

STEAM SEPARATLY, EACH IN FRESH WATER, UNTIL TENDER BUT STILL SOMEWHAT CHISP

250 g (1/2 lb) red potatoes, sliced
2 C cauliflower, cut in flowerets
1 medium carrot, cut in 5cm x 6 mm (2 x 1/4 inch) sticks
125 g (1/4 lb) green beans, cut in 5 cm (2 inch) pieces
2 C cabbage, shredded
1 C Chinese white radish, sliced, or cucumber
500 g (1 lb) bean sprouts

ARRANGE IN LAYERS; CABBAGE, CARROTS, CAULIFLOWER, BEANS, AND BEAN SPROUTS. ARRANGE RADISH AND POTATO SLICES AROUND THE EDGES.

GARNISH WITH

2 eggs, hard cooked and sliced
6 cherry tomatoes
1 1/2 C firm tofu, cut in 1.3 cm (1/2 inch) cubes
2 scallions, shredded

CHILL THE VEGETABLE PLATTER IN A FRIDGE.

MAKE A SAUCE BY COMBINEING IN A SAUCEPAN

1 C thick coconut milk
1/3 C crunchy peanut butter
2 garlic cloves, chopped finely
3 T soy sauce
3 T lemon juice
1 piece lemon rind, 2.5 cm (1 inch) square
3 T brown sugar
1 T dried red pepper, crushed
1/2 tsp salt
2 T water

BRING TO A BOIL OVER MODERATE HEAT. LOWER HEAT AND SIMMER UNTIL THICK. POUR OVER THE VEGETABLES OR SERVE SEPARATELY.

## CUCUMBER COCONUT SALAD

PEEL, CUT INTO SLICES, AND PUT IN A BOWL

2 cucumbers

SPRINKLE WITH

salt

LEAVE FOR FIVE MINUTES, RINSE, AND DRAIN.

ADD

3 T lime juice

4 fresh chillies, shredded (2 red 2 green)

1 medium onion, sliced thinly

MIX AND ADD

3/4 C coconut milk

CHILL, TOSS, AND SERVE.

## CARROT SALAD

IN A BOWL MIX

4 C carrots, grated

1/4 C raisins

4 T sugar

3 T vinegar

1 T vegetable oil

1/2 tsp salt

1/4 tsp black pepper, ground

LET MARINATE IN FRIDGE 8 HOURS, MIXING OCCASIONALLY.

## CUCUMBER TOMATO YOGURT SALAD

PEEL

2 cucumbers

CUT IN QUARTERS LENGTHWISE, REMOVE SEEDS AND SLICE 3mm (1/8 inch) THICK. COMBINE IN A BOWL WITH

4 T onion, chopped finely

ADD

2 tomatoes, cut in 1.3 cm (1/2 inch) cubes

ADD A MIXTURE OF

1 C yogurt

1 1/2 tsp cumin powder

1/2 tsp garam masala

1 fresh hot green chilli pepper, chopped finely

MIX THOROUGHLY AND LET SIT IN A REFRIGERATOR, COVERED, FOR 1 HOUR OR MORE, AND SERVE.
BEST WITH CHICKEN CURRY

## CHINESE CUCUMBER SALAD

CUT
1 large cucumber
INTO 7.6 cm (3 inch) LONG BY 1.3 cm (1/2 inch) WIDE STICKS. PUT IN A COLLANDER, IN A BOWL, AND SPRINKLE WITH
2 tsp salt
LET STAND 15 MINUTES. RINSE, PAT DRY, AND SET ASIDE.
COMBINE IN A BOWL
1 T shallots, chopped finely
2 tsp garlic, chopped finely
2 tsp soy sauce
2 T white wine, or rice vinegar
2 tsp sugar
2 fresh chillies, chopped finely
1 T sesame oil
ADD THE CUCUMBER, MIX, MARINATE FOR 10 MINUTES AND SERVE.

VARIATION

LEAVE OUT CHILLIES AND ADD TO DRESSING
1 tsp sichuan peppercorns, ground
1 tsp hot bean sauce

## BEAN SPROUT SALAD

MAKE AN OMELET OF
2 eggs, beaten lightly
SHRED AND PLACE IN A LARGE MIXING BOWL.
INTO A COLANDER PUT
4 C bean sprouts
OVER THEM POUR
4 L (4 quarts) boiling water
DRAIN, COOL, AND ADD THE SPROUTS TO THE BOWL.
ADD
1 cucumber, shredded
1 C roast pork, diced
IN A SAUCEPAN COMBINE
1/3 C soy sauce
5 fresh green chillies, sliced thinly (optional)
2 tsp sesame oil
1 1/2 tsp sugar
BRING TO A BOIL, REMOVE FROM HEAT, AND LET COOL.
IN ANOTHER BOWL COMBINE
2/3 C black vinegar, or plain vinegar
1 1/2 T ginger, chopped
1/2 tsp salt
TO THE BEAN SPROUT MIXTURE ADD 2 T OF THE SOY SAUCE MIXTURE, AND 1/4 C OF THE VINEGAR MIXTURE. TOSS WELL. USE THE REMAINING SAUCES AS DIPS. SERVE WITH RICE NOODLES.

## FENNEL AND CUCUMBER SALAD

WASH AND DICE

1 cucumber

PUT THE CUCUMBER IN A COLLANDER IN LAYERS, SPRINKLING EACH LAYER WITH

Salt

PUT A SAUCER ON TOP TO WEIGH THE CUCUMBER DOWN AND LET SIT ABOUT 30 MINUTES. RINSE AND PAT DRY. MEANWHILE TRIM AND CLEAN

2 fennel bulbs

DISCARD THE TOUGH STALKS BUT RETAINING SOME OF THE FEATHERY ENDS, IF AVAILABLE. CUT INTO SLICES AND PUT THE FENNEL INTO A BOWL WITH THE CUCUMBER.

DRESSING

IN A BOWL MIX

1 T lemon juice
1 T olive oil
1 T fresh mint, chopped
1 tsp sugar

AND BEAT UNTIL WELL BLENDED. ADD THE DRESSING TO THE VEGETABLES AND TOSS GENTLY, BUT THOUROUGHLY. SERVE ON

Lettuce leaves

This is simple but very good. Combine it with Greek Fried Squid (page 173) and Tzatzeki Sauce (page 64), and you have a real experience.

## GREEK VILLAGE SALAD

PLACE IN A BOWL

3 tomatoes, cut in wedges
1 onion, sliced thinly and rings separated
1/4 C feta cheese, cut into 1.3 cm (1/2 inch) cubes
1 tsp dried oregano
10 black olives
salt
pepper

TOSS AND DRESS WITH

2 T lemon juice
1/4 C olive oil

## NGAIRE'S PASTA SALAD

COOK AND DRAIN

500 gr (1 pound) pasta

MIX IN

1/3 C olive oil

THEN ADD

1/3 C white wine vinegar
1 T fresh basil leaves, chopped finely
1/4 C parsley, chopped finely
1/4 tsp black pepper, ground
1/2 tsp salt
2 shallots, chopped finely

TOSS WELL AND ADD

100 gm (1/4 pound) mozzarella cheese, cubed
10 black olives, sliced
1 small zucchini, sliced
1 tomato, cut in wedges

TOSS AGAIN TO MIX.

## GERMAINE'S POTATO SALAD

STEAM
6 potatoes, cut in 2.5 cm (1 inch) cubes
WHEN TENDER REMOVE TO A BOWL AND DRIZZLE WITH
vinegar
ADD
1/2 tsp garlic powder
1/4 C scallions, chopped
1/4 C parsley, chopped
ADD AND MIX IN
mayonnaise, or salad dressing, to taste
TOSS AND REFRIGERATE. BEFORE SERVING DRIZZLE WITH
vinegar
olive oil

## BEAN SALAD

DRAIN AND MIX IN A BOWL
400 ml (14 oz) Can cut green beans
400 ml (14 oz) Can wax beans
400 ml (14 oz) Can kidney beans
400 ml (14 oz) Can garbonzo beans, (chick peas)
ADD
1 onion, diced
1 green sweet bell pepper, diced
IN ANOTHER BOWL, MIX
1/3 C sugar
1/2 C vinegar
1/2 C vegetable oil
1 tsp salt
1/2 tsp black pepper, ground
ADD THIS TO BEANS AND STIR IN. REFRIGERATE 24 HOURS, MIXING OCCASIONALLY.

## CREAMY DILL CUCUMBER DRESSING OR DIP

IN A BLENDER MIX

1 C yogurt
1/2 cucumber
1/2 green pepper
1 small onion
1/2 tsp salt
1/2 tsp dried dill

BLEND UNTIL SMOOTH
USE ON SALADS, OR AS A DIP.

## YOGURT DIJON SALAD DRESSING

MIX

1 C plain yogurt
1 T Dijon mustard
3 T lemon juice
1/2 tsp salt
1 garlic clove, chopped finely

## FRENCH DRESSING

IN A SMALL SAUCEPAN COMBINE

1 T corn starch
3/4 tsp salt
Pinch black pepper, ground
1 1/2 C water
1/2 C vinegar
1/4 C lemon juice
2 T vegetable oil
3 garlic cloves, chopped finely
2 T ketchup

BRING TO A BOIL OVER MEDIUM HEAT, STIRRING CONSTANTLY. LOWER HEAT AND SIMMER 1 MINUTE. LET COOL AND SERVE ON SALADS.

# SAUCES AND CHUTNEYS

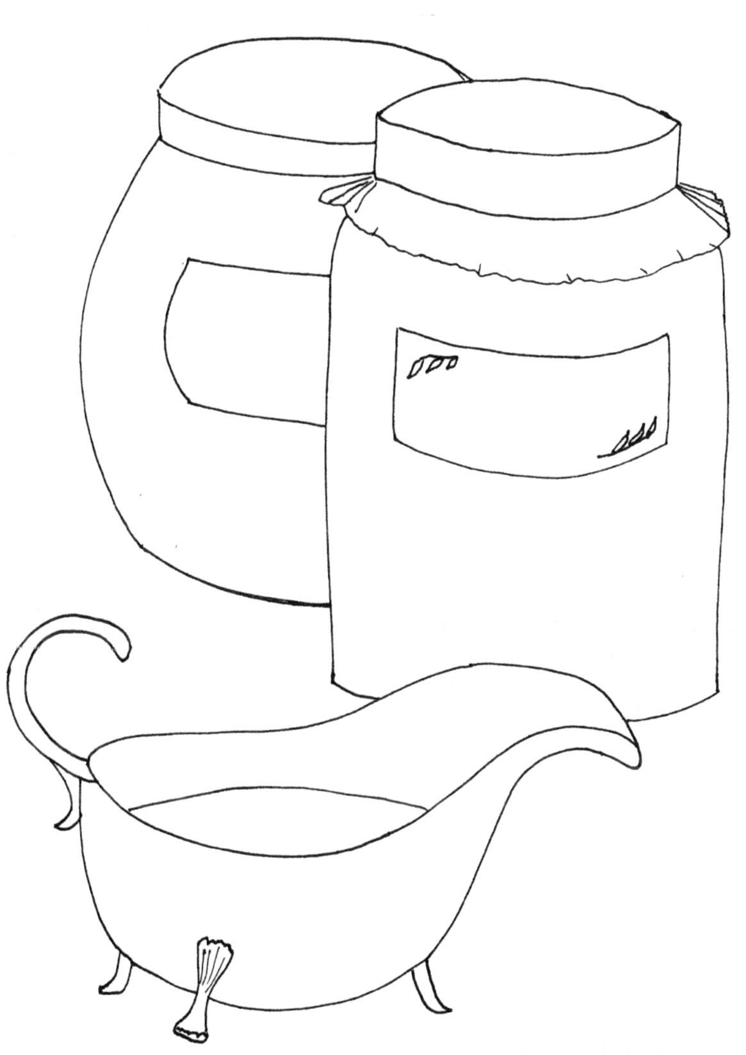

## HONEY STIR FRY SAUCE

MIX TOGETHER

2 scallions, chopped finely
1 T vegetable oil
1 T honey
3 T tomato ketchup
2 T soy sauce
1 tsp French mustard

USE THE SAUCE AS A DIP, OR ADD TO A STIR FRY NEAR THE END OF COOKING.

## TZATZIKI SAUCE

DRAIN THROUGH MUSLIN CLOTH, SUSPENDED OVER A BOWL, FOR AT LEAST 2 HOURS

1 C plain yogurt

PLACE THE YOGURT IN A BOWL AND ADD

1 cucumber, chopped finely
2 garlic cloves, chopped finely
1 T olive oil
1 T lemon juice
1 tsp dried dill, or 1 T fresh, chopped
1/2 tsp dried oregano, or 2 T fresh, chopped, (mint can be substituted)
1/2 tsp salt
1/4 tsp black pepper

MIX THOUROUGHLY. LET SIT FOR 1 HOUR AND SERVE WITH VEGETABLES, FISH, OR MEATS.

## OREGANO LEMON SAUCE FOR LAMB OR FISH

IN A SAUCEPAN HEAT
2 T olive oil
ADD, AND FRY UNTIL TRANSLUCENT
1 medium onion, chopped finely
ADD
1 T dried oregano
1/2 tsp salt
1/2 tsp red pepper powder
4 T lemon juice
MIX AND SIMMER 10 MINUTES. SERVE ON THE SIDE.

## MARION BERRY SAUCE FOR CHICKEN

IN A SAUCEPAN HEAT
1 C marion berries (or blackberries)
AND ADD
2 T lemon juice
1/4 C chicken stock, or water
BRING TO A SIMMER AND ADD A MIXTURE OF
2 tsp corn starch
1T water
RAISE HEAT AND BOIL UNTIL THICKENED. SERVE WITH GRILLED CHICKEN.

# HOISIN BBQ SAUCE

IN A BOWL MIX

2 C ketchup
1/4 C Dijon mustard
3 T light corn syrup
3 T hoisin sauce
3 T lemon juice
2 T vinegar
1 tsp red pepper powder
1 tsp lemon zest
4 garlic cloves, chopped finely

REFRIGERATE UNTIL USED.

This Chinese based recipe came about by choosing part of the original to be used as a basting sauce for barbecuing chicken.

## HUNAN STRANGE FLAVORED CHICKEN BBQ SAUCE

COMBINE IN A BOWL

1 tsp chilli oil, or 1/2 tsp red pepper powder
2 tsp Sichuan peppercorns, toasted in a dry frying pan and ground
1 T sesame oil
1 1/2 T peanut oil
2 T soy sauce
1 tsp salt
2 T wine vinegar
1 T sesame paste (tahini), or peanut butter
1 T sugar
1 tsp fresh ginger, grated
2 scallions, chopped, including greens

MIX WELL AND ALLOW TO SIT TO BLEND FOR A FEW HOURS BEFORE USING. BRUSH ON CHICKEN AS IT COOKS, OR USE AS A SAUCE, COOKED A BIT, AS A DIP, OR ON A SALAD.

This won first place one year in the local agricultural fair. Kathryn makes it using overgrown zucchini, sometimes 50 cm (1 1/2 feet) long from the garden. Zucchini actually refers to a small squash but who is nitpicking. Great for hamburgers.

## ZUCCHINI CONFETTI RELISH

IN A LARGE BOWL COMBINE

8 C zucchini, chopped
2 C onions, chopped
1/2 C green bell pepper, chopped
1 C red bell pepper, chopped

SPRINKLE WITH

1/4 C pickling salt

STIR AND LET STAND 1 TO 2 HOURS, STIRRING OCCASIONALLY. DRAIN, RINSE THOROUGHLY UNDER COLD WATER, AND DRAIN AGAIN. PRESS OUT EXCESS MOISTURE.

IN A LARGE POT COMBINE

1 1/2 C sugar
1 1/2 C pickling vinegar
1 1/2 tsp dry mustard
1 tsp celery seeds
1/2 tsp black pepper, coarsely ground
1/2 tsp turmeric powder

BRING TO A BOIL. ADD THE DRAINED VEGETABLES AND RETURN TO A BOIL, STIRRING OFTEN. LOWER HEAT. SIMMER UNCOVERED UNTIL VEGETABLES ARE TENDER AND SAUCE IS THICK.

IN A SMALL BOWL STIR TOGETHER

2 tsp corn starch
1 T water

AND ADD TO RELISH. COOK UNTIL CLEAR, ABOUT 5 MINUTES, STIRRING CONSTANTLY. LADLE INTO HOT STERILIZED JARS AND SEAL IMMEDIATELY.

I developed this to use up a large part of my garden bounty near the end of summer. The ingredients from the garden include all the chillies, large and small, tomatoes, shallots, garlic, and parsley

## REAL GOOD TOMATO SALSA

IN A LARGE POT MIX

4 large hot chilli peppers, such as Hungarian hot wax, deseeded and diced
2 T fresh parsley, chopped
2 1/2 C shallots, chopped well
20 garlic cloves, chopped
12 C tomatoes, diced (1.3 cm (1/2 inch))
1/2 C tomato paste
4 T pickling vinegar
4 T vegetable oil
4 jalapeno or green serrano chilli peppers, cut into 1.3 cm (1/2 inch) pieces
1 T pickling salt
1/2 tsp cumin powder
1/2 tsp coriander powder

BRING TO A BOIL AND SIMMER 10 TO 20 MINUTES, OR UNTIL THICK. IF MIXTURE IS TOO THIN BRING TO A BOIL AND SLOWLY ADD, WHILE STIRRING, A MIXTURE OF

1 T corn starch
1 T water

COOK UNTIL CLEAR. REMOVE FROM HEAT AND PUT IN HOT STERILIZED JARS. SEAL IMMEDIATELY.

## FRESH TOMATO LIME SALSA

COMBINE

5 medium tomatoes, sliced
1/3 C onion, chopped
4 garlic cloves, chopped finely
4 fresh green chilli peppers, chopped finely
1/2 tsp salt
2 T lime juice
3 T cilantro (fresh coriander leaves), snipped

MIX WELL AND SERVE.

This is likely a very old British recipe, passed down through Diana Knowles, through the Stanier family, and based on Indian chutneys.

## TOMATO RELISH

PEEL, CORE, AND COARSELY CHOP
1.5 kg (3 lb) tomatoes
SPRINKLE WITH
1/2 C pickling salt
COVER AND LET STAND OVERNIGHT.
IN A LARGE POT COMBINE TOMATOES WITH
4 large onions, coarsely chopped
2 1/2 C pickling vinegar
BRING TO A BOIL AND SIMMER 10 MINUTES.
ADD
2 C sugar
10 fresh red chilli peppers, chopped
COOK UNTIL SUGAR IS DISSOLVED AND SIMMER 5 MINUTES.
IN A SMALL BOWL COMBINE
1 T curry powder
1 T turmeric powder
1 1/2 tsp dry mustard
1 tsp cumin powder
1 tsp fenugreek, ground
2 T all purpose flour
Water, enough to make a paste
ADD CURRY MIXTURE TO TOMATO MIXTURE, STIRRING TO AVOID LUMPS. SIMMER 1 1/2 HOURS, STIRRING OCCASIONALLY. PUT IN STERILIZED JARS AND SEAL AT ONCE.

This recipe was adopted to use the often large crop of peaches from my peach tree.

## PEACH CHUTNEY

COMBINE IN A POT

4 tsp red pepper powder
12 peaches, cut in wedges
2 C brown sugar
3 garlic cloves, chopped finely
2 C pickling vinegar
1 C raisins
2 T fresh ginger, grated
1 tsp cinnamon powder
1 T yellow mustard seeds
6 green cardamom pods, ground
2 T lemon juice
1 T pickling salt

BRING TO A BOIL AND THEN LOWER HEAT. SIMMER 1 HOUR. PUT IN STERILIZED BOTTLES, AND SEAL AT ONCE.

This is another Stanier family recipe, again likely of old British origin, based on Indian chutneys.

## TOMATO CHUTNEY

GRIND IN A MINCER

2 large onions
2 kg (4 lb) tomatoes
2 kg (4 lb) apples
500 g (1 lb) sultana (blond) raisins
2 whole lemons

TO THE MINCE ADD

2 T pickling salt
2 C pickling vinegar
2 T red pepper powder

SIMMER 4 HOURS. PUT IN STERILIZED BOTTLES AND SEAL AT ONCE.

## RHUBARB CHUTNEY

INTO A LARGE POT PUT

2 kg (4 lb) rhubarb, chopped
1 kg (2 lb) dates, or raisins, chopped
2 medium onions, chopped finely
4 tomatoes, peeled and chopped
2 C pickling vinegar
1 1/2 C brown sugar
1 T fresh ginger, ground
2 T mustard seeds
4 tsp pickling salt
1 tsp red pepper powder

BRING TO A BOIL AND SIMMER 1 HOUR. PUT IN STERILIZED BOTTLES AND SEAL AT ONCE.

This is a standard to be served with north African dishes. Very good but use sparingly.

## HARISSA

IN A BOWL MIX

250 g (1/2 lb) fresh chillies, chopped finely
1 head garlic,(10 large cloves), peeled and chopped finely
1 T coriander powder
1 T caraway seeds, crushed
3 T fresh mint, chopped finely
3 T cilantro (fresh coriander leaves), chopped finely
1 T salt
1 T olive oil, or more, to make a paste

PUT IN A SMALL POT AND SIMMER A FEW MINUTES OR MICROWAVE UNTIL WELL HEATED. REFRIGERATE IF PASTE IS GOING TO BE USED SOON AFTER. FREEZE TO KEEP FOR EXTENDED PERIODS. THE PASTE IS VERY HOT.

# CHILLI SAUCE

GRIND
25 hot red peppers, fresh or dry
PUT IN A BOWL AND ADD
1/4 C pickling vinegar
MIX CHILLIES IN TO SOAK.
ADD
1 T ginger, grated
8 garlic cloves, put through a press
MIX AND LET STAND.
INTO A SAUCEPAN PUT
1 3/4 C pickling vinegar
HEAT AND ADD
1/2 C sugar
MIX UNTIL SUGAR IS DISSOLVED AND ADD
2 T pickling salt
MIX AND ADD THE CHILLI MIXTURE. BRING TO A BOIL, LOWER HEAT, AND SIMMER 5 MINUTES. LET COOL AND STRAIN THROUGH A SIEVE, SCRAPING AS MUCH CHILLI FLESH THROUGH AS YOU CAN. PUT SIEVED MIXTURE BACK INTO THE SAUCEPAN AND BRING TO A BOIL.
ADD A MIXTURE OF
1 T corn starch
1 T water
BRING BACK TO A BOIL AND BOIL UNTIL THICKENED.
PUT IN A STERILIZED BOTTLE AND REFRIGERATE.

Another use for all my excess greenhouse chillies.

## CHILLI GARLIC SAUCE

IN A SAUCEPAN MIX TOGETHER
4 heads garlic, peeled and chopped finely
1 T salt
16 fresh chilli peppers, chopped finely
1/4 C lemon juice
1/4 C vinegar
BRING TO A BOIL, LOWER HEAT, SIMMER 5 MINUTES, SERVE WITH SOUP ETC. KEEPS WELL IN A FRIDGE.

## CARIBBEAN HABANERO SAUCE

INTO A SAUCEPAN PUT
1/2 C onion, chopped
4 garlic cloves, chopped
1/2 C carrots, chopped
FRY UNTIL ONION IS SOFT AND ADD
1/4 C water
SIMMER UNTIL CARROT IS SOFT AND ADD
12 habanero chillies, chopped, use rubber gloves. These are the hottest chilli.
SIMMER 2 MINUTES AND BLEND IN A FOOD PROCESSOR UNTIL SMOOTH.
RETURN TO THE POT AND ADD
1/2 C pickling vinegar
1/4 C lime juice
SIMMER 5 MINUTES, STRAIN, AND PACK IN SMALL JARS.
MAKES 1 1/2 CUPS.

## OREGANO CHILLI SAUCE
## (FOR MEATS OR VEGETABLES)

PLACE IN A SAUCEPAN

2 medium tomatoes, chopped
2 tsp dried oregano
3 garlic cloves, chopped finely
1/4 tsp salt
1/2 tsp chilli oil, or 1/4 tsp red pepper powder

BRING TO A BOIL AND SIMMER AT LEAST 30 MINUTES. SERVE WITH SAUSAGES OR VEGETABLES.

## CHILLI OIL

IN A SAUCEPAN HEAT

2 C peanut oil or vegetable oil

UNTIL IT JUST SMOKES. REMOVE FROM HEAT AND ADD, KEEPING YOUR FACE AWAY FROM POT

1 C dried red chilli peppers, crushed
1 T Sichuan peppercorns, crushed (optional)
2 tsp fresh ginger, grated(optional)

ALLOW TO COOL TO ROOM TEMPERATURE. COVER TIGHTLY AND LET SIT 24 HOURS. STRAIN THROUGH CHEESECLOTH AND PUT IN A SEALED JAR.

# MEATS

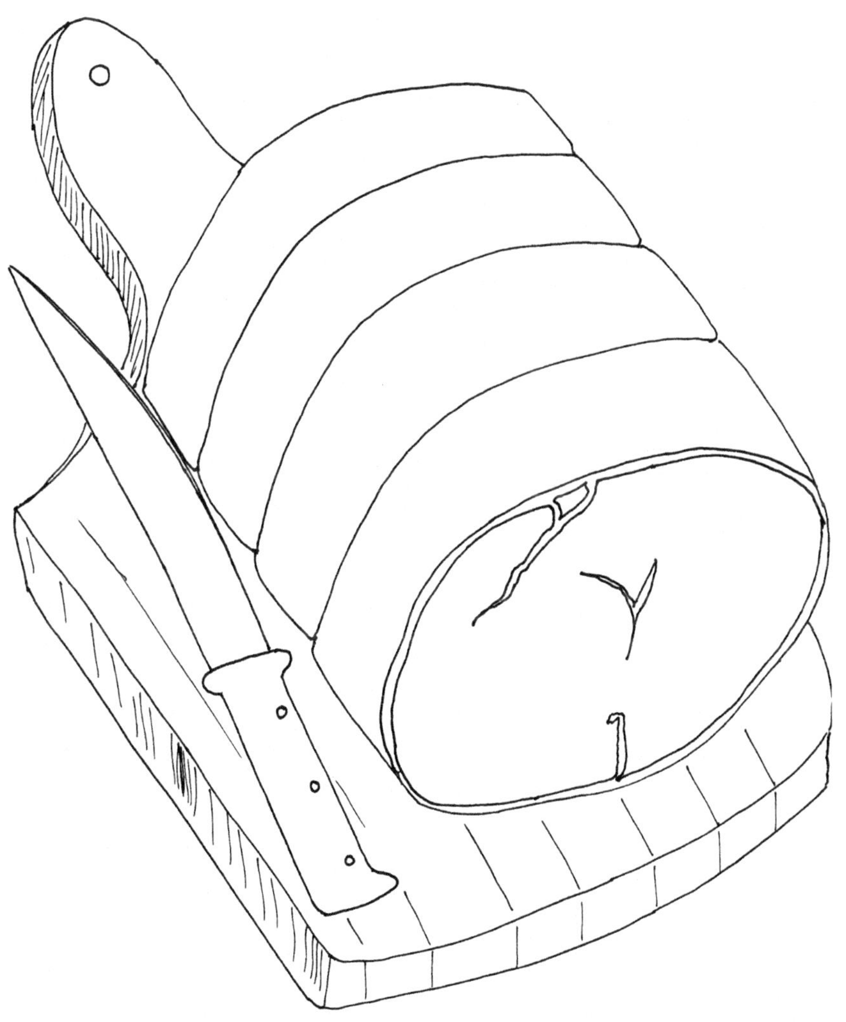

## BEEF BURRITO

IN A POT BROWN

500 g (1 lb) lean ground beef

DRAIN, IF NECESSARY, ANDADD

3 garlic cloves, chopped finely

1 medium onion, chopped finely

FRY, STIRRING, FOR 5 MINUTES, AND ADD

1/2 C Real Good Tomato Salsa (page 69), or commercial salsa

1/2 tsp cumin powder

1 tsp salt

1/2 tsp red pepper powder

MIX AND ADD

1 C refried beans, or cooked mashed potatoes

MIX THOROUGHLY AND HEAT THROUGH.

HAVE EACH PERSON MAKE THEIR OWN.

SERVE WITH

Soft flour tortillas

1 Can chillies, diced

Lettuce, shredded

Tomatoes, chopped

Cheese, grated

Avocado, chopped or sliced

## MEATLOAF

(180 C (350 F) - 1 hour)
(20 cm x 25 cm (8x10 inch) ovenproof baking dish)

IN A FRYING PAN HEAT
1 T olive oil
ADD
1 medium onion, chopped
AND FRY UNTIL TRANSLUCENT.
PLACE THE ONION IN A BOWL AND ADD
500 g (1 lb) ground beef
6 garlic cloves, chopped
MIX AND ADD
1 C bread crumbs
1 1/2 T fresh parsley, chopped
1 T Worcestershire sauce
1/2 tsp salt
1/2 tsp black pepper, ground
1 tsp dried oregano
2 eggs
MIX WELL AND PLACE IN THE BAKING DISH, PRESSING DOWN. BAKE AS ABOVE.

## HAMBURGER PATTIES

USE THE MEATLOAF RECIPE, ABOVE, BUT LEAVE OUT BREAD CRUMBS.

## HOISIN GROUND BEEF

IN A LARGE FRYING PAN FRY UNTIL LIGHT BROWN
2 medium onions, chopped
3 T garlic, chopped finely
1/2 tsp fresh ginger, grated
ADD
1 T thick black bean sauce
1 T hoisin sauce
1/2 tsp red pepper powder
MIX AND ADD
500 g (1 lb) ground beef
LOWER HEAT AND COOK UNTIL BEEF IS DONE AND MOISTURE REDUCED.

## FIVE SPICE GROUND BEEF

IN A LARGE POT HEAT

1 T vegetable oil

2 tsp sesame oil

ADD

500 g (1 lb) ground beef

2 C onions, chopped finely

125 g (1/4 lb) button mushrooms, diced (optional)

FRY UNTIL THE BEEF IS JUST COOKED.

IN A SMALL BOWL MIX

3 T soy sauce

4 garlic cloves, finely chopped

1/4 tsp red pepper powder

1/2 tsp five spice powder

1 tsp ginger juice

ADD TO THE BEEF MIXTURE AND ADD

3 C water

MIX WELL AND BRING TO A BOIL, LOWER HEAT TO LOW, AND SIMMER 25 TO 30 MINUTES.

ADD, AND MIX IN, 5 MINUTES BEFORE SERVING

2 tsp sesame oil

A tasty way to use beef sausages.

## BEEF SAUSAGE WITH OREGANO POTATOES

INTO A FRYING PAN PLACE

10 large beef sausages, cut in three, or 750 g (1 1/2 lb) meat balls

FRY AT HIGH HEAT TO BROWN AND ADD

2 large onions, chopped coarsely

2 tsp dried oregano

LOWER HEAT AND ADD

1/2 C water

SIMMER FOR 45 MINUTES, STIRRING OCCASIONALLY.

MEANWHILE, BOIL

4 potatoes.

FOR 20 MINUTES.

REMOVE, DRAIN, AND CUT INTO 1 INCH CUBES.

REMOVE SAUSAGES TO A BOWL OR PLATE WHEN DONE.

DRAIN THE ONIONS WELL AND RETURN TO THE PAN.

FRY ON HIGH FOR A FEW MINUTES TO DRY SLIGHTLY AND ADD THE POTATOES AND SAUSAGE. STIR TO COAT THE POTATOES AND SERVE.

This is my favorite chili recipe. Using fresh tomatoes is best, but works well with canned tomatoes.

## CHILI CON CARNE

INTO A LARGE POT PUT

500 g (1 lb) ground beef

COOK UNTIL COLORED AND DRAIN OFF FAT.

ADD AND FRY, STIRRING, UNTIL TRANSLUCENT

1 medium onion chopped
5 garlic cloves, minced

ADD

1 500 ml (19oz) Can kidney beans, drained and rinsed
3 large tomatoes, chopped
2 T tomato paste
3/4 tsp salt
1/2 tsp black pepper, ground
1 tsp red pepper powder, or more
1 1/2 tsp dried oregano
1/2 tsp coriander powder

BRING TO A BOIL AND LOWER HEAT. SIMMER 1 HOUR.

## SAFE GOULASCH

IN A POT HEAT

2 T vegetable oil

ADD

2 1/2 C medium onion, chopped

FRY UNTIL TRANSLUCENT AND ADD

1kg (2 lb) stewing beef

FRY UNTIL BROWNED A LITTLE AND ADD

1 T sweet paprika

1 tsp all purpose flour

2 garlic cloves, chopped

1 T tomato paste

1 tsp salt

1/4 tsp caraway seed, ground

1/2 tsp dried marjoram

1/2 C water

SIMMER UNTIL THE MEAT IS TENDER AND SERVE WITH BOILED POTATOES AND SALAD.

## GREEK ONION AND BEEF STEW

IN A FRYING PAN HEAT

1/4 C olive oil

ADD AND BROWN

750 g (1 1/2 lb) stewing beef, cut in 2.5 cm (1 inch) cubes

REMOVE THE BEEF FROM THE PAN. TO THE PAN ADD AND BROWN

1 large onion, sliced in rings

5 garlic cloves, chopped finely

ADD

1/2 tsp salt

1/2 tsp black pepper, ground

1/2 tsp allspice, grated

1/2 tsp sugar

1 cinnamon stick 5 cm (2 inches) long

1 1/3 C dry red wine

750 g (1 1/2 lb) tomatoes, chopped

1/4 C tomato paste

STIR WELL AND ADD THE BEEF. BRING TO A BOIL, REDUCE HEAT TO SIMMER, AND COVER. COOK 2 HOURS, STIRRING OCCASIONALLY. SERVE WITH BUTTERED PASTA OR RICE.

## DURANGO BEEF STEW

GRIND FINELY AND SET ASIDE

2 poblano chillies

IN A FRYING PAN HEAT

1 T oil

ADD

500 g (1 lb) stewing beef, cut into 1.3 cm (1/2 inch) cubes

BROWN QUICKLY OVER HIGH HEAT. REMOVE THE BEEF, AND PLACE IT IN A LARGE POT, AND RESERVE.

TO THE FRYING PAN ADD

1 large onion, finely chopped
3 garlic cloves, finely chopped

FRY UNTIL TENDER AND ADD TO THE BEEF IN THE POT.

TO THE FRYING PAN ADD

1 medium tomato, chopped

COOK FOR 5 MINUTES AND ADD TO THE POT.

ADD THE RESERVED CHILLIES TO THE POT AND

1 C beef stock, or water, or enough to cover
1 tsp salt
1/2 tsp black pepper, ground
1/2 tsp dried oregano

BRING TO A BOIL, REDUCE HEAT AND SIMMER UNTIL MEAT IS TENDER, ABOUT 2 HOURS. ADD AND MIX IN, SHORTLY BEFORE SERVING

1 T lemon juice

## CHINESE BEEF BLACK BEAN STEW

IN A LARGE POT HEAT

2 T vegetable oil

ADD AND FRY UNTIL LIGHTLY BROWNED

1 kg (2 lb) beef, cut in 2.5 cm (1 inch) cubes

ADD

1 large onion, sliced

FRY UNTIL LIGHTLY BROWNED AND ADD

3 T fermented black beans, rinsed and chopped coarsely

4 garlic cloves, chopped finely

3 dried red pepper flakes

2 tsp ginger, grated

STIR FOR 3 MINUTES AND ADD

1 C beef, or chicken, broth

1/4 C sherry

1 tsp sugar

1/4 C soy sauce

4 carrots, cut in diagonal slices 3 mm (1/8 inch) thick

2 potatoes, cubed

6 water chestnuts, sliced

1 C peas

BRING TO A BOIL, LOWER HEAT, AND SIMMER UNTIL BEEF IS TENDER. BRING BACK TO A BOIL AND THICKEN WITH A MIXTURE OF

1 T corn starch

2 T water

ADD GRADUALLY TO THE STEW, STIRRING CONSTANTLY, UNTIL THICKENED. REMOVE FROM HEAT.

## COLUMBIAN BEEF STEW

IN A CASSEROLE HEAT

2 T olive oil

ADD

1/2 C onion, chopped

COOK 4 TO 5 MINUTES, STIRRING CONSTANTLY, UNTIL TRANSLUCENT.

STIR IN

2 medium tomatoes, chopped

2T tomato paste

COOK 3 MINUTES AND ADD

1 kg (2 lb) stewing beef

1 bay leaf

1 tsp cumin powder

2 tsp dried oregano

1/4 tsp turmeric, powder

3 garlic cloves, chopped

2 tsp salt

10 black peppercorns, whole

3 C cold water

2 tsp cider vinegar

1/4 tsp red pepper powder

REDUCE HEAT TO LOW AND SIMMER 1 TO 2 HOURS.
SERVE WITH VEGETABLES AND POTATOES, EITHER SEPARATELY OR COOKED IN THE STEW.

## MEXICAN BEEF STEW

IN A LARGE POT COMBINE

750 g (1 1/2 lb) lean stewing beef
1 large onion, sliced
3 garlic cloves
4 T olive oil
3 T wine vinegar
1/2 C tomato sauce, or 1 tomato, chopped
1 C red wine
2 tsp dried oregano
1 bay leaf
1/2 tsp salt
1/4 tsp black pepper, ground
1 C Real Good Tomato Salsa (page 69), or commercial salsa

BRING TO A BOIL, STIRRING OCCASIONALLY. REDUCE HEAT AND SIMMER UNTIL THE MEAT IS TENDER.

## BEEF CURRY STEW

IN A LARGE POT HEAT

2 T vegetable oil

AT MEDIUM HIGH AND ADD

1 kg (2 lb) stewing beef, cubed

FRY UNTIL BROWN ON ALL SIDES.

ADD

1 large onion, chopped

STIR UNTIL BROWNED.

LOWER HEAT, ADD AND STIR IN

1 T curry powder

1/2 tsp cinnamon powder

COOK, STIRRING, FOR 5 MINUTES, AND ADD

1/2 C tomato juice

1 tsp salt

1 C water

BRING TO A BOIL, REDUCE HEAT, AND SIMMER 45 MINUTES, STIRRING OCCASIONALLY.

ADD

6 medium carrots, cubed

6 medium potatoes, cubed

SIMMER 45 MINUTES LONGER, OR UNTIL ALL IS TENDER.

MAKE A MIXTURE OF

1/4 C cold water

2 T all purpose flour

STIR INTO STEW UNTIL THICKENED.

# MALAYSIAN COCONUT BEEF CURRY

POUND, OR BLEND TO A PASTE IN A FOOD PROCESSOR

1 C onion, chopped
4 garlic cloves, chopped finely
1 T fresh ginger, grated
1 tsp red pepper powder
2 tsp lemon zest
1/2 tsp coriander powder
2 tsp salt

IN A POT HEAT

2 T oil

ADD AND LIGHTLY BROWN

1/2 C dried flaked coconut,

ADD THE SPICE ONION PASTE AND

1 kg (2 lb) beef, cut in 2.5 cm (1 inch) cubes

STIR UNTIL BEEF IS WELL COATED AND FRY 5 MINUTES.
ADD

2 C coconut milk
1 T sugar
2 T lemon juice

SIMMER 45 MINUTES, ADDING WATER IF NECESSARY.
SAUCE SHOULD BE THICK BUT NOT DRY.

## CHINESE CURRIED BEEF

IN A POT HEAT

3 T vegetable oil

BROWN

750 g (1 1/2 lb) beef, cut in 2.5 cm (1 inch) cubes

REMOVE THE BEEF AND SET ASIDE.

TO THE POT ADD

2 garlic cloves chopped

2 dried red peppers crushed

1 medium onion, cut in 2.5 cm (1 inch) cubes

STIR FRY 1 MINUTE

ADD

1 medium potato cut in 2.5 cm (1 inch) cubes

STIR 30 SECONDS AND ADD

3 T curry powder

MIX WELL, RETURN THE BEEF TO THE POT, AND ADD

1/4 tsp five spice powder

1 1/2 T wine

2 tsp sugar

3/4 tsp salt

1 T soy sauce

1 1/4 C beef stock, or water

MIX WELL AND BRING TO A BOIL. REDUCE HEAT AND SIMMER UNTIL BEEF IS TENDER, ABOUT 2 HOURS.

## CHINESE RED COOKED BEEF

TO A MEDIUM POT ADD

3 C water<br>
1 C soy sauce<br>
4 T sherry, or rice wine<br>
2 fresh ginger slices, 3 mm (1/8 inch) thick<br>
2 garlic cloves, chopped<br>
1 tsp five spice powder<br>
2 tsp sesame oil<br>
2 T brown sugar

BRING TO A BOIL AND ADD

1 kg (2 lb) beef, in one piece, or cut in 4 cm (1 1/2 inch) cubes

SIMMER FOR 3 HOURS IF ONE PIECE, OR UNTIL TENDER.
TURN OCCASIONALLY IF THE MEAT IS NOT COVERED.
ALLOW MEAT TO COOL IN THE LIQUID.

## CHINESE DRY FRIED SHREDDED BEEF WITH GREEN BEANS

SHRED

250 g (1/2 lb) beef, raw or cooked

INTO 5 cm x 3 mm (2 x 1/4 inch) SHREDS AND PLACE IN A BOWL.

ADD

1 T soy sauce

1 tsp sesame oil

1 T dry sherry or rice wine

MARINATE FOR 20 MINUTES OR LONGER, STIRRING OCCASIONALLY.

IN A FRYING PAN HEAT

2 T vegetable oil

AND ADD

3 garlic cloves, chopped finely

2 dried red peppers, cut in half lengthways, including seeds

3 fresh ginger slices, 3 mm (1/8 inch) thick, cut in half

STIR FRY CHILLIES AND GINGER A FEW MINUTES UNTIL FLAVORS ARE ABSORBED BY THE OIL, AND ADD THE BEEF MIXTURE. FRY UNTIL ALL MOISTURE IS ABSORBED BY THE MEAT AND ADD

2 C green beans, whole

FRY, STIRRING FREQUENTLY, UNTIL BEANS ARE TENDER.

## SICHUAN DRY FRIED SHREDDED BEEF

HEAT A FRYING PAN AND ADD

2 T Oil

RAISE THE HEAT TO HIGH AND ADD

500 g (1 lb) lean beef, cut in 5 cm by 3mm (2 inch by 1/4 inch) shreds

1 T wine

STIR UNTIL THE SHREDS SEPARATE AND REDUCE HEAT.

POUR OFF ANY EXCESS LIQUID AND STIR UNTIL THE BEEF IS DRY.

STIR IN

1 T hot bean paste

1 T hoisin sauce

1 garlic clove, finely chopped

1/2 tsp salt

1 T sugar

1 T rice wine or dry sherry

STIR TO THOROUGHLY COAT THE MEAT.

INCREASE HEAT TO HIGH AND ADD

3 large carrots, cut in 3 mm by 5 cm (1/8 by 2 inch) shreds

AND STIR FRY 1 MINUTE.

ADD

2 scallions, finely chopped

2 tsp ginger, grated

1/2 tsp Sichuan peppercorns, ground

1 tsp chilli oil, or 1/2 tsp red pepper powder

STIR FRY 1 MINUTE.

## BEEF WITH TOMATO AND ONION

CUT AGAINST THE GRAIN
500 g (1 lb) beef
INTO 5 x 2.5 cm x 6 mm (2 x 1 x 1/4 inch) THICK STRIPS.
IN A FRYING PAN HEAT
3 T vegetable oil
AND ADD THE BEEF WITH
2 T soy sauce
1 tsp cornstarch
2 T scallions, chopped
2 tsp fresh ginger, grated
1/2 tsp sugar
Pinch black pepper, ground
STIR FRY 1 1/2 TO 2 MINUTES. REMOVE THE BEEF AND RESERVE.
TO FRYING PAN ADD
1 onion, sliced
COOK UNTIL TENDER AND ADD
2 tomatoes, cut in wedges
STIR UNTIL HEATED THROUGH. ADD THE BEEF AND MIX WELL.

# KOREAN BRAISED SHORT RIBS

SOAK
5 dried black mushrooms
FOR 25 MINUTES. DRAIN THE MUSHROOMS, SQUEESING TIGHTLY TO REMOVE EXCESS WATER. CUT INTO QUARTERS, DISCARDING THE STEMS. STIR FRY THE MUSHROOMS IN VEGETABLE OIL FOR TWO MINUTES AND SET ASIDE.
IN A BOWL MIX
1 medium onion, chopped
4 garlic cloves, finely chopped
5 scallions, chopped
AND SET ASIDE.
INTO ANOTHER BOWL PUT
1 kg (2 lbs) beef short ribs, trimmed of fat
2 T sugar
KNEAD FOR ONE MINUTE AND ADD
1 tsp sesame oil
KNEAD FOR 2 MINUTES AND SET ASIDE.
PUT THE BEEF INTO A POT WITH THE ONION MIXTURE AND ADD
3 C water
2 T soy sauce
BRING TO A BOIL, LOWER HEAT, COVER, AND COOK OVER MODERATE HEAT FOR 1 HOUR.
ADD THE MUSHROOMS AND
2 T soy sauce
2 tsp sesame oil
1 tsp salt
125 g (1/4 lb) Chinese white radish, cut in 2.5 cm (1 inch) cubes, (optional)
10 Chinese chestnuts, (optional)
SIMMER FOR A FURTHER HALF HOUR, ADDING WATER IF NECESSARY.

This tastes infinitely better than it sounds. I had my doubts the first time I tried it but was very pleasantly surprised.

## PORTUGESE PORK WITH CLAMS

IN A LARGE POT HEAT
1/4 C olive oil
ADD
1 kg (2 lb) lean pork, cut in 2.5 cm (1 inch) cubes
FRY UNTIL BROWN AND ADD
1 lb chorizo sausage, or (Garlic Sausage and 1/2 tsp red pepper powder)
FRY 1 TO 2 MINUTES AND ADD
125 g (1/4 lb) prosciutto ham, diced, or bacon, or other cured ham
FRY A FEW MINUTES AND ADD
3 medium onions, chopped
8 garlic cloves, chopped
BROWN, WHILE STIRRING, AND THEN ADD
2 bay leaves
2 tsp paprika
1/2 C fresh parsley, chopped finely
1/2 C cilantro (fresh coriander leaves), chopped finely
1 tsp red pepper powder
2 tsp lemon juice
3/4 C dry white wine
COOK UNTIL THE WINE IS REDUCED BY HALF AND ADD
6 tomatoes, chopped
COVER AND SIMMER 45 MINUTES.
JUST BEFORE SERVING ADD
40 clams, in their shell, or 2 350 ml (12oz) Cans clams.
COOK, COVERED, UNTIL THE CLAMS OPEN, DISCARDING ANY UNOPENED ONES.
IF USING CANED CLAMS SIMMER UNTIL THEY ARE WELL HEATED.

## PORK STIR FRY

MARINATE FOR AT LEAST 30 MINUTES
500 g (1 lb) pork, cut in 1.3 cm (1/2 inch) cubes
IN A MIXTURE OF
1/4 C soy sauce
3 T sherry, or rice wine
5 slices fresh ginger, 3 mm (1/8 inch) thick.
8 garlic cloves, chopped finely
REMOVE MEAT FROM MARINADE AND FRY IN A LARGE POT, OR WOK, UNTIL BROWNED.
ADD, AND STIR FRY, IN ORDER OF TIME NEEDED TO COOK
Vegetables, of your choosing
NEAR END OF COOKING ADD
1 T sesame oil
TO THICKEN SAUCE, SLOWLY ADD A MIXTURE OF
1 T corn starch
1 T water
STIR UNTIL THICKENED AND INGREDIENTS ARE COATED.

## GREEK GRILLED PORK CHOPS

MARINATE
4 pork chops
IN A MIXTURE OF
2 garlic cloves, mashed
4 T olive oil
2 tsp dried oregano
2 T lemon juice
FOR 2 HOURS. GRILL, TURNING ONCE, SPRINKLING WITH
Salt
Black pepper, ground

## PORK WITH CHILLIES

TO A MEDIUM SIZE BOWL ADD AND MIX

3 dried red peppers, crushed
1 C tomato sauce
2 garlic cloves, chopped finely
1 small onion, chopped finely
1/2 tsp salt
3 C water

IN A FRYING PAN HEAT

2 T vegetable oil

ADD AND BROWN

1 kg (2 lb) lean pork, cut to bite size pieces

SPRINKLE WITH

Salt
Black pepper, ground

LOWER HEAT AND ADD

4 T all purpose flour

MIX, RAISE HEAT, ADD CHILLI TOMATO MIXTURE TO THE PORK, AND STIR UNTIL IT COMES TO A BOIL. TURN HEAT LOW AND SIMMER 35 TO 45 MINUTES, STIRRING OCCASIONALLY.

## PORK CHOPS WITH BLACK BEAN SAUCE

(180 C (350 F) 1 hour)

RINSE AND DRY

6 pork chops

RUB THEM WITH A MIXTURE OF

1 tsp five spice powder

1/2 tsp red pepper powder, (optional)

1 tsp salt

PLACE THE CHOPPS IN A BAKING DISH.

IN A BOWL MIX TOGETHER

1/2 C thin black bean sauce, or 1 T thick bean sauce

4 scallions, chopped

4 garlic cloves, chopped finely

1/4 C wine, or sherry

2 T soy sauce

1/4 C water

POUR OVER THE CHOPS. COVER THE BAKING DISH WITH FOIL AND BAKE AS ABOVE, TURNING CHOPS TWICE.

This is the first recipe I tried using fermented black beans. It was an instant hit. I discovered that it was the only way the kids liked broccoli, so broccoli with black beans was often made.

## PORK WITH BLACK BEANS AND BROCCOLI

CUT INTO 2.5 cm (1 inch) CUBES AND RESERVE
375 g (3/4 lb) lean pork
CUT UP AND RESERVE
500 g (1 lb) broccoli, or cabbage, or chard
IN A POT, OR WOK, HEAT
2 T vegetable oil
ADD
4 garlic cloves, finely chopped
1 tsp red pepper powder
1 T fresh ginger, grated
STIRR FRY 2 MINUTES, ADD THE PORK, AND STIRR FRY 2 MINUTES LONGER. REMOVE THE PORK AND ADD
2 T fermented black beans, rinsed and chopped
STIR A FEW SECONDS, ADDING MORE OIL IF NECESSARY.
ADD
2 T soy sauce
1 tsp sugar
ADD THE BROCCOLI AND STIR FRY TO COAT WITH OIL.
ADD
1/2 tsp black pepper, ground
1/4 C chicken stock, or water
COVER AND COOK 3 MINUTES. UNCOVER, RETURN THE PORK AND STIR FRY UNTIL DONE.
ADD
2 tsp sesame oil
1 T soy sauce
MIX UNTIL ALL IS WELL COATED. THICKEN SAUCE WITH A MIXTURE OF
1 T corn starch
1 T water
SERVE HOT

## INDONESIAN BRAISED PORK

IN A FRYING PAN HEAT

3 T oil

ADD AND BROWN

750 g (1 1/2 lb) pork, cut in 1.3 cm (1/2 inch) cubes

ADD

3/4 C onion, chopped finely

2 garlic cloves, chopped finely

1/2 tsp red pepper powder

STIR FREQUENTLY FOR 10 MINUTES AND ADD

1/3 C soy sauce

1 tsp lemon juice

2 tsp brown sugar

SIMMER 10 MINUTES AND SERVE.

## SWEET AND SOUR PORK

IN HOT OIL, IN A FRYING PAN, BROWN

750 g (1 1/2 lb) lean pork, cut into 2.5 cm (1 inch) cubes,

LOWER HEAT AND FRY UNTIL JUST COOKED.

ADD

1 C pineapple chunks

1/4 C pineapple Juice

COVER AND SIMMER 10 MINUTES. SET ASIDE.

IN A SMALL POT COMBINE

4 T corn starch

6 T sugar

4 T soy sauce

6 T vinegar

1/2 C pineapple juice

BRING TO A BOOIL AND COOK, STIRRING CONSTANTLY, UNTIL CLEAR. POUR OVER THE MEAT MIXTURE AND SIMMER 5 MINUTES. SERVE OVER NOODLES OR RICE.

This is a very nice way to prepare pork, and the Ti Malice Sauce can be used in many other ways.

## HAITIAN GLAZED AND BRAISED PORK WITH TI-MALICE SAUCE

IN A HEAVY FRYING PAN HEAT

3 T vegetable oil

OVER MODERATE HEAT UNTIL A LIGHT HAZE FORMS.

ADD

1 kg (2 lb) lean pork, cut into 5 cm (2 inch) cubes

BROWN STIRRING UNTIL DRY.

ADD, STIRRING IN

1 medium onion, finely chopped
1 T shallots, finely chopped
1 1/2 C orange juice, strained
3 T lime juice, strained
1/4 tsp dried thyme, (optional)
1/2 tsp salt
1/2 tsp black pepper, ground

BRING TO A BOIL OVER HIGH HEAT AND COVER THE PAN. LOWER HEAT AND SIMMER 30 MINUNTES. UNCOVER THE PAN AND RAISE THE HEAT TO HIGH. COOK, STIRRING FREQUENTLY, TO PREVENT MEAT FROM STICKING, UNTIL THE SAUCE THICKENS TO A GLAZE. SERVE WITH TI-MALICE SAUCE, WHICH FOLLOWS.

## TI-MALICE SAUCE

FINELY CHOP
1 medium onion
AND PUT IT INTO A BOWL.
STIR IN
1/2 C lime juice, strained
MARINATE AT ROOM TEMPERATURE FOR AT LEAST 30 MINUTES. DRAIN THE ONIONS, REMOVING AS MUCH LIQUID AS POSSIBLE, RESERVING THE MARINADE.
IN A FRYING PAN HEAT
1 T butter
OVER MODERATE HEAT.
WHEN FOAM BEGINS TO SUBSIDE ADD THE MARINATED ONIONS AND COOK, STIRRING FREQUENTLY, UNTIL TRANSLUCENT.
STIR IN
1 tsp red pepper powder
1 tsp garlic, finely chopped
REDUCE HEAT TO LOW, COVER PAN, AND COOK FOR 15 MINUTES. REMOVE FROM HEAT AND STIR IN THE RESERVED MARINADE.
ADD
1 1/2 tsp salt
STIR WELL AND COOL TO ROOM TEMPERATURE.
SERVE IN A SEPARATE BOWL WITH THE HAITIAN GLAZED AND BRAIZED PORK.

# SICHUAN SAUTEED PORK

MARINATE FOR 30 MINUTES OR MORE

500 g (1 lb) pork, cut in 1.3 cm (1/2 inch) cubes

IN A MIXTURE OF

3 T soy sauce
3 T wine
1 1/2 tsp sugar
2 1/2 tsp sesame oil
1 T corn starch

WHEN READY TO COOK HEAT IN A FRYING PAN

2 T vegetable oil

ADD

1 T fresh ginger, shredded
4 garlic cloves, chopped
1 1/2 tsp dried red peppers, crushed
3/4 tsp Sichuan peppercorns, crushed

STIR FOR 15 SECONDS AND ADD THE MARINATED PORK.
FRY, STIRRING, 2 TO 3 MINUTES, ADDING

Water, as needed to prevent drying.

ADD

1 medium onion, cubed
2 tsp hot bean paste, or hot chilli sauce
1/4 C water, or soup stock

BRING TO A BOIL AND ADD A MIXTURE OF

2 tsp water
2 tsp corn starch

COOK, STIRRING, UNTIL THICKENED.

## PORK IN CHINESE BARBECUE SAUCE

INTO A BOWL PUT

750 g (1 1/2 lb) pork, cut in 2.5 cm (1 inch)cubes

ADD A MIXTURE OF

2 T rice wine, or sherry
3 T sugar
2 T soy sauce
1/2 tsp five spice powder
1 tsp salt

MIX WELL AND MARINATE 2 HOURS, TURNING PORK OCCASIONALLY.

IN A POT HEAT

3 T peanut, or vegetable oil

AND ADD

3 scallions, finely chopped
2 tsp fresh ginger, grated
5 garlic cloves, finely chopped

STIR FRY A FEW SECONDS AND ADD THE PORK, DRAINED, RESERVING THE MARINADE. FRY UNTIL BROWNED. REMOVE PORK AND VEGETABLES WITH A SLOTTED SPOON AND POUR OFF EXCESS OIL. PLACE RESERVED MARINADE IN THE POT AND HEAT THROUGH. RETURN PORK AND VEGETABLES TO THE POT AND COOK GENTLY UNTIL SAUCE IS QUITE THICK AND ABSORBED BY THE MEAT.

## SPARE RIBS ALOHA

IN A SHALLOW BAKING DISH, AT 230 C (450 F) FOR 1 HOUR BAKE

1.5 kg (3 lb) pork spareribs

REMOVE FROM THE OVEN AND POUR OFF THE FAT

MEANWHILE, FOR THE SAUCE, IN A BOWL MIX

1/2 C onion, chopped finely
1/2 C green sweet bell pepper, chopped finely
1C tomato sauce
2 garlic cloves, chopped finely
1/2 tsp dried oregano
1 1/2 tsp dried basil
1 T Worcestershire sauce
1/3 C vinegar
2 1/2 C pineapple chunks, including juice
1/4 C brown sugar
1/2 tsp dry mustard
Salt
Black pepper, ground

POUR THE SAUCE OVER THE RIBS AND REDUCE HEAT TO 180 C (350 F). BAKE 1 1/2 HOURS, BASTING FREQUENTLY.

## FINGER LICKIN COUNTRY RIBS

(190 C (375 F) 3 hours total)

IN A BOWL COMBINE

2 medium onions, cut into thick rings
2/3 C soy sauce
4 T red wine vinegar
1/2 C honey
2 tsp black pepper, coarsely ground
2 tsp fresh ginger, grated
1/2 tsp red pepper powder
1 1/2 tsp garlic powder
2 T dry mustard

POUR THE MIXTURE OVER

2 kg (4 lb) lean pork spareribs

WHICH HAVE BEEN PLACED IN A LARGE BAKING DISH. COAT ALL THE RIBS. TURN FREQUENTLY, AS THEY MARINATE, FOR 6 HOURS. REMOVE THE RIBS, RESERVING THE MARINADE, AND PLACE THEM ON A RACK IN THE BAKING DISH. BAKE UNCOVERED 45 MINUTES. REMOVE SPERERIBS, AND RACK, AND DRAIN DISH. RETURN THE RIBS TO THE BAKING DISH,WITHOUT THE RACK. POUR THE MARINADE OVER THE RIBS. BAKE, COVERED, FOR 1 HOUR. REMOVE THE COVER AND BAKE 1 HOUR, BASTING AND TURNING THE RIBS FREQUENTLY IN THE SAUCE.

## SPARERIBS IN BLACK BEAN SAUCE

CUT

1.5 kg (3 lb) pork spareribs

INTO SECTIONS AND CUT EACH SECTION INTO 5 cm (2 INCH) LENGTHS. THIS WILL REQUIRE A GOOD HEAVY CLEAVER AND A VERY SOLID SURFACE. BROWN THE RIBS IN A WOK OR LARGE POT IN TWO BATCHES.

TO THE SECOND BATCH ADD

3 T fermented black beans, rinsed and chopped

4 garlic cloves, chopped

REMOVE RIBS AND SET ASIDE.

INTO THE LARGE POT OR WOK PUT

1 1/2 T soy sauce

3 T sherry, or rice wine

1 tsp sugar

1 slice fresh ginger 3 mm (1/8 inch) thick

1/2 C water

MIX WELL AND ADD THE RIBS. BRING TO A BOIL, LOWER HEAT, AND SIMMER FOR ONE HOUR.

NEAR THE END ADD

1 tsp sesame oil

RAISE HEAT AND THICKEN SAUCE WITH

1 T corn starch

2 T water

## POLYNESIAN SHISH-KA-BABS

MARINATE

1 kg (2 lb) pork, cut in 2.5 cm (1 inch) cubes

FOR 2 HOURS IN A MIXTURE OF

1 T lime or lemon juice
1 T soy sauce
1 pinch turmeric powder
1 pinch coriander powder
1 tsp sugar
2 garlic cloves, chopped finely

SKEWER ALTERNATELY WITH

Onion, cut in 2.5 cm (1 inch) pieces
Tomatoes, cut in wedges
Sweet green bell pepper, cut in 2.5 cm (1 inch) pieces

BROIL. HEAT PEANUT-CHILLI SAUCE (page 124) AND SERVE AS A DIP.

## SOUVLAKIA

IN A LARGE BOWL COMBINE

1 kg (2 lb) lean pork, cut in 2.5 cm (1 inch) cubes
1/4 C olive oil
2 T lemon juice
Salt
1/2 tsp black pepper, ground
2 tsp dried oregano
4 bacon strips, cut in half
4 small tomatoes, quartered
2 onions, sliced thickly
1 sweet green bell pepper, cut in 2.5 cm (1 inch) pieces

MARINATE IN REFRIGERATOR, COVERED, FOR SEVERAL HOURS, MIXING OCASIONALLY.

SKEWER PIECES ALTERNATELY.

GRILL FOR 15 MINUTES, TURNING 3 OR 4 TIMES. BASTE WITH RESERVED MARINADE. SERVE WITH LEMON WEDGES, RICE, TZATZIKI (page 64), AND GREEK SALAD. (page 58)

## SPANISH PORK BRAISED WITH CILANTRO AND LEMON

CUT INTO 2.5 cm ( 1 inch) CUBES

1 kg (2 pounds) lean pork

IN A LARGE FRYING PAN, OR POT, HEAT

2 T olive oil

FRY THE PORK ON HIGH HEAT TO BROWN, STIRRING FREQUENTLY.

ADD AND STIR IN

3/4 C dry white wine, or water
2 tsp cumin powder
3 garlic cloves, chopped finely
1/2 tsp black pepper, ground
1 tsp salt

BRING TO A BOIL, COVER, LOWER HEAT, AND SIMMER FOR 25 MINUTES, OR UNTIL THE PORK IS TENDER.

ADD

1/4 C dry white wine
1/2 lemon, sliced thinly and each slice quartered

COOK ON HIGH, STIRRING CONSTANTLY, UNTIL THE SAUCE BEGINS TO THICKEN.

STIR IN

2 T cilantro (fresh coriander leaf), chopped

AND SERVE.

## PORK AND PEPPERONI STEW

IN A LARGE POT HEAT

2 T olive oil

ADD AND FRY UNTIL TRANSLUCENT

1 large onion, chopped

ADD

1 1/2 C pepperoni sausage, chopped in 1.3 cm (1/2 inch) pieces
1 1/2 C pork, chopped in 1.3 cm (1/2 inch) cubes
2 C broccoli, cut in pieces
2 tsp dried oregano
1 tsp salt
1 tsp black pepper, ground
4 medium potatoes, cut in cubes
3 medium tomatoes, chopped
1 C chicken stock or water, or enough to cover

BRING TO A BOIL, REDUCE HEAT, AND SIMMER 45 MINUTES.

## GREEK LAMB STEW

IN A FRYING PAN HEAT

1 T olive oil

2 T butter, or margarine

AT MEDIUM HIGH UNTIL THE BUTTER MELTS.

ADD

600 g (1 1/4 lb) lamb, cut into 2.5 cm (1 inch) cubes

AND BROWN. REMOVE THE LAMB FROM THE PAN AND RESERVE.

TO THE PAN ADD

1 medium onion, quartered and separated

AND FRY UNTIL LIMP.

ADD

1/2 C tomato sauce

1/4 C ketchup

1/2 C white wine

1/4 C water

1 tsp dried oregano

1/2 tsp salt

1/4 tsp black pepper, ground

3 carrots, sliced

RETURN THE BROWNED MEAT TO THE PAN. MIX WELL AND REDUCE HEAT. SIMMER 1 1/2 HOURS OR UNTIL LAMB IS TENDER.

## MOUSSAKA

THINLY SLICE

1 large eggplant, or 3 small

PLACE IN A BOWL AND SALT SLICES. LET STAND FOR ONE HOUR. SQUEEZE, RINSE, AND PAT DRY. FRY QUICKLY IN

2 T olive oil

REMOVE' AND DRAIN ON ABSORBENT PAPER AND RESERVE. IN A FRYING PAN HEAT

2 T olive oil

ADD

2 medium onions, thinly sliced

FRY UNTIL GOLDEN AND ADD

Pinch salt
Pinch black pepper, ground
750 g (1 1/2 lb) ground lamb, or beef

FRY UNTIL WELL BROWNED AND ADD

1/2 tsp allspice, grated
1 tomato, chopped
2 T tomato paste
3 T fresh parsley, chopped

SIMMER FOR 15 TO 20 MINUTES. IN A DEEP BAKING DISH PLACE ALTERNATE LAYERS OF EGGPLANT AND ONION MIXTURE, STARTING AND ENDING WITH EGGPLANT. IN A SAUCEPAN MAKE A WHITE SAUCE WITH

4 T butter, melted
4 T all purpose flour
2 C hot milk
Pinch nutmeg, grated
Salt
Black pepper, ground
2 eggs beaten

SIMMER UNTIL SAUCE THICKENS. POUR SAUCE OVER THE CONTENTS OF THE BAKING DISH. BAKE AT 180 C (350 F) FOR 45 MINUTES, UNTIL THE TOP IS BROWNED WELL, AND THE LAYERS ARE BLENDED.

# LAMB IN CHILLI VINEGAR SAUCE

INTO A HEAVY POT, PUT

1.5 kg (3 lb) lamb, cut in 4 cm (1 1/2) inch cubes
1 medium onion, chopped
1 garlic clove, chopped finely
3 cilantro sprigs(fresh coriander), finely chopped, or parsley
1 tsp salt
Water to barely cover

BRING TO A BOIL AND SIMMER UNTIL THE MEAT IS TENDER, ABOUT 1 1/2 HOURS. DRAIN THE LAMB, STRAIN THE STOCK AND RESERVE THE LIQUID. RINSE AND DRY THE POT, AND RETURN THE LAMB TO IT.

IN A BOWL BLEND TO A PASTE

3 fresh red chilli peppers, chopped finely
1 garlic clove, chopped finely
1/8 tsp cumin powder
1/2 tsp dried oregano
2 T wine vinegar
Salt

IN A FRYING PAN HEAT

3 T vegetable oil

COOK THE PASTE, STIRRING CONSTANTLY, FOR ABOUT 5 MINUTES. POUR THE RESERVED STOCK OVER THE LAMB IN THE POT AND ADD THE PASTE. SIMMER ON LOW HEAT, UNCOVERED FOR 20 MINUTES.

This was tried just for fun one day and has become one of my favorite, quick to prepare, meals.

## LAMB WITH TOMATOES

(180 C (350 F) - 1 hr.)

PLACE
1kg (2 lb) lamb chops
IN THE BOTTOM OF A BAKING DISH AND COVER WITH
Tomato slices
SPRINKLE WITH
1 tsp dried oregano, (preferably Greek)
1/2 tsp red pepper powder
1/2 tsp black pepper, ground
Pinch salt
SEAL WITH ALUMINUM FOIL AND BAKE AS ABOVE.

## LAMB CURRY

IN A LARGE POT HEAT
2 T vegetable oil
AND ADD
2 large onions, chopped
4 garlic cloves, chopped finely
1 T fresh ginger, grated
FRY UNTIL ONION IS SOFT AND GOLDEN.
ADD
2 T curry powder
2 tsp salt
2 T lemon juice
AND MIX THOROUGHLY.
ADD
1 kg (2 lb) lean lamb, cubed
STIR CONSTANTLY UNTIL COATED WELL AND ADD
3 large tomatoes, chopped
2 fresh chilli peppers, chopped finely
2 T fresh mint leaves, chopped finely
1 tsp garam masala
2 T fresh parsley, chopped finely, or cilantro (fresh coriander leaf)
BRING TO A BOIL, REDUCE HEAT, AND SIMMER 1 HOUR AND 45 MINUTES, OR UNTIL THE LAMB IS TENDER.

## MOROCCAN MEATBALLS IN TOMATO SAUCE

MIX AND WORK TO A SMOOTH PASTE

1 kg (2 lb) ground lamb
2 medium onions, grated
2 garlic cloves, finely chopped
1 T fresh parsley finely chopped
1 T cilantro (fresh coriander leaf), finely chopped
1 tsp cumin powder
1 tsp cinnamon powder
1/2 tsp fresh ginger, finely chopped
1tsp salt
1 tsp black pepper, ground

ROLL INTO SMALL BALLS AND SET ASIDE.

INTO A LARGE SKILLET PLACE

2 T olive oil

HEAT AND ADD

750 g (1 1/2 lb) tomatoes, peeled and chopped

COOK UNTIL SOFTENED AND ADD

3 dried chilli peppers, crushed
1 T fresh parsley, chopped
1/2 tsp cumin powder
1/2 tsp cinnamon powder
1 tsp red pepper powder, (can be omitted)

ADD THE MEATBALLS TO THE SAUCE AND ADD

Water, enough to cover

SIMMER GENTLY 30 to 40 MINUTES.

## VARIATION (CURRIED TOMATO MEATBALLS)

PROCEED AS MOROCCAN MEATBALLS, BUT REPLACE THE MEATBALL HERBS AND SPICES, EXCEPT THE GARLIC, WITH 1 1/2 T CURRY POWDER. REPLACE THE SAUCE HERBS AND SPICES WITH 1/2 tsp RED PEPPER POWDER.

This dish is very spicy hot, but very good.

## BROILED MEAT WITH PEANUT CHILLI SAUCE

### PEANUT CHILLI SAUCE

IN A FRYING PAN HEAT
1 T peanut oil
ADD
4 garlic cloves, chopped finely
1 tsp fresh ginger, grated
3 shallots, chopped finely
FRY FOR 3 TO 4 MINUTES AND ADD
1 C chicken stock, or water
BRING TO A BOIL, REDUCE HEAT, AND ADD
1 T dried red peppers, crushed
1 T soy sauce
2 tsp brown sugar
1/4 tsp cumin powder
1 T lime juice
1/2 C crunchy peanut butter
MIX WELL AND REMOVE 1/2 C FOR THE BEEF AND SIMMER UNTIL THICKENED.

### BEEF

MARINATE,
500 g (1 lb) beef, lamb or pork, cut in 2.5 cm (1 inch) cubes
IN A MIXTURE OF 1/2 CUP OF THE ABOVE MIXTURE AND
2 T lime juice
FOR AT LEAST 2 HOURS, MIXING OCASIONALLY.
THREAD THE MEAT ON SKEWERS AND GRILL, BASTING WITH REMAINING MARINADE ONCE. USE THE COOKED SAUCE AS A DIP FOR MEAT OR RAW VEGETABLES.

# POULTRY AND STUFFINGS

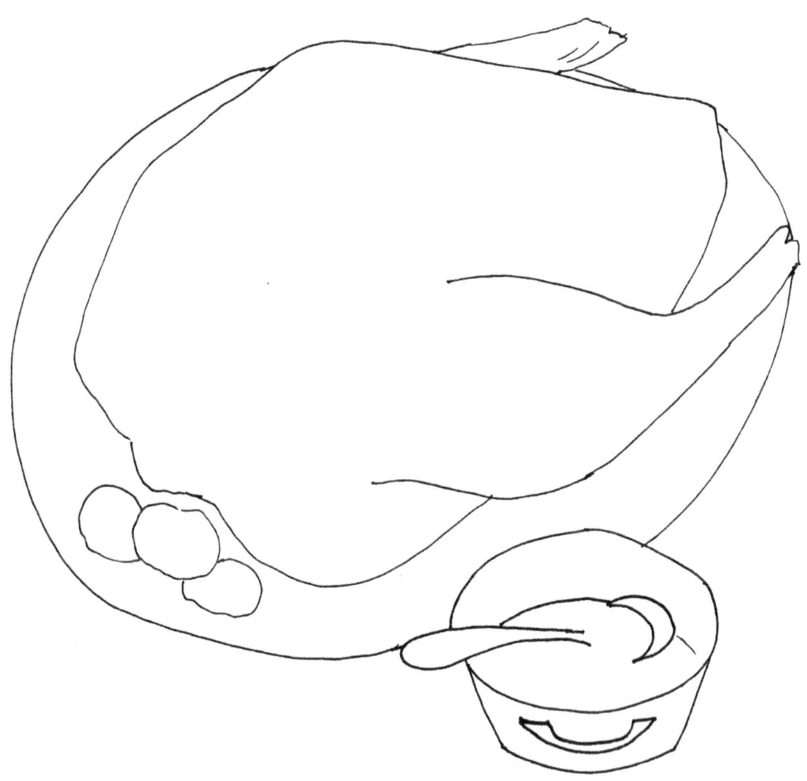

## CHICKEN CACCIATORE

DREDGE
1.5 kg (3 lb) chicken, cut up
IN
All purpose flour
IN A FRYING PAN HEAT
2 T vegetable oil
BROWN THE CHICKEN, REMOVE, AND RESERVE.
INTO THE PAN PUT
1/2 C carrot, sliced
1/2 C onion, sliced
3 garlic cloves, chopped
FRY 2 MINUTES AND ADD
2 C tomatoes, chopped
2 T fresh parsley, chopped
1 tsp dried basil
1 tsp salt
1/4 tsp black pepper, ground
1/4 C dry red wine, (optional)
RETURN THE CHICKEN AND SIMMER FOR 15 MINUTES.
ADD
1 C button mushrooms, sliced
SIMMER ANOTHER 15 MINUTES.

You could call this an Indian burrito since the filling is essentially a thickened curry.

## SPICED CHICKEN OR TURKEY
## BURRITO FILLING

IN A LARGE POT COMBINE

1/2 C chicken broth
1 T lemon juice
1/2 tsp black pepper, ground
1/2 tsp red pepper powder

BRING TO A BOIL AND ADD

3 C chicken, or turkey, cubed, raw or cooked,

SIMMER 15 MINUTES OR UNTIL MEAT IS DONE.
MEANWHILE, COMBINE IN A SAUCEPAN

1/2 C mayonnaise
1/2 C plain yogurt
6 scallions, chopped
1/4 C fresh parsley, chopped
1 tsp turmeric powder
1 tsp cumin powder
1 tsp corn starch
4 T chicken broth, or water

SIMMER UNTIL THICKENED AND ADD THE YOGURT MIXTURE TO THE CHICKEN MIXTURE. COMBINE WELL AND FILL

Tortillas

## CHINESE LEMON CHICKEN

FOR THE BRAISING LIQUID, IN A LARGE POT MIX

4 T soy sauce
4 T sherry, or (white wine plus 1 T sugar)
1 tsp sugar
2 garlic cloves, sliced
1 slice fresh ginger, 3mm (1/8 inch) thick
3/4 tsp sesame oil
2 whole star anise
2 dried red peppers, broken in half, with seeds
1/2 C chicken broth, or water

IN A FRYING PAN HEAT

1 1/2 T vegetable oil

BROWN

1.5 kg (3 lb) chicken, chopped in small pieces, with bones

WHEN ALL THE CHICKEN IS BROWNED TRANSFER IT TO THE BRAISING LIQUID. BRING TO A BOIL AND REDUCE HEAT. SIMMER UNTIL THE CHICKEN IS DONE, ABOUT 35 TO 40 MINUTES.

MEANWHILE, COMBINE IN A SAUCEPAN

3/4 C lemon juice
Zest of 1 lemon, finely grated
3/4 C sugar

COOK OVER LOW HEAT UNTIL SUGAR DISSOLVES, STIRRING.CONSTANTLY.

SIMMER 10 MINUTES AND THEN STIR IN A MIXTURE OF

2 tsp corn starch
2 tsp water

COOK,STIRRING UNTIL THE LEMON SAUCE THICKENS. REMOVE THE CHICKEN FROM THE BRAISING LIQUID, WHICH MAY BE REUSED, AND PUT IT IN A SERVING BOWL. POUR THE SAUCE OVER THE CHICKEN, OR SERVE SEPARATELY. SPRINKLE THE CHICKEN WITH

Scallion, sliced into rings

This has to be one of my very favorite ways to prepare chicken. The procedure is a bit convoluted, but the result is so good you will always want more.

## THE BEST LEMON CHICKEN

IN A LARGE BOWL MARINATE

2 chicken breasts, skinned and cut into 2.5 cm (1 inch) cubes

FOR 1 HOUR, OR UP TO 24 HOURS COVERED IN THE REFRIGERATOR, IN A MIXTURE OF

1/4 tsp sugar
1/2 tsp corn starch
1/2 tsp soy sauce
1/2 tsp dry sherry, or white wine
1/2 tsp sesame oil
1 tsp water

IN A BOWL COMBINE THE FOLLOWING SEASONING LIQUID

3 T sugar
3 T lemon juice
3/4 C pineapple juice, unsweetened
1/2 tsp sesame oil

SET ASIDE.

IN A CUP COMBINE THE FOLLOWING THICKENER

2 T corn starch
4 T water

SET ASIDE.

IN A SAUCEPAN HEAT

1 T vegetable oil

ADD

2 garlic cloves, chopped finely
1 T fresh ginger, grated
1 tsp fermented black beans, rinsed and coarsely chopped
Zest of one lemon
1 tsp red pepper powder

COOK, STIRRING, 30 SECONDS AND ADD THE SEASONING LIQUID JUICES. BRING TO A BOIL AND ADD THE THICKENER, STIRRING UNTIL THICK, AND SET ASIDE.

MAKE A BATTER OF

1/2 C all purpose flour
1/4 C corn starch
1 tsp baking powder
1/2 tsp baking soda
1/8 tsp salt

MIX AND ADD

1/2 C water
1 T vegetable oil

STIR UNTIL JUST COMBINED WITHOUT OVER MIXING.
MIX CHICKEN INTO BATTER, INCLUDING THE MARINADE.
USE A TABLESPOON TO LIFT OUT CHICKEN PIECES.
DEEP FRY IN BATCHES
SERVE WITH THE SEASONING SAUCE.

## LEMON PEPPER CHICKEN

IN A LARGE SKILLET HEAT

2 T vegetable oil

ADD

1 frying chicken, skinned and cut up

AND FRY UNTIL BROWN, ABOUT 15 MINUTES.
SPRINKLE WITH

3 T lemon juice
1 tsp black pepper, ground

ADD

1/4 C water

BRING TO A BOIL AND LOWER HEAT. COVER AND SIMMER 30 MINUTES, TURNING CHICKEN TWICE. ADD MORE WATER IF NECESSARY. REMOVE COVER, RAISE HEAT, AND REDUCE SAUCE UNTIL THICK.

## GREEK LEMON OREGANO CHICKEN

(190 C (375 F) - 45 minutes)

CUT INTO SERVING PIECES
1.5 kg (3 lb) chicken
IN A BOWL COMBINE
1 T dried oregano
1/2 tsp salt
1/4 tsp black pepper, ground
1/4 C olive oil
2 T lemon juice
ADD CHICKEN TO THE MARINADE AND MARINATE ONE HOUR, STIRRING 3 OR 4 TIMES. PLACE CHICKEN ON RACK IN A PAN AND BAKE AS ABOVE, BASTING OCCASIONALLY.

## LEMON GARLIC CHICKEN

FRY UNTIL LIGHTLY BROWNED
8 pieces chicken, skinned
ADD
10 garlic cloves, coarsely chopped
FRY 3 MINUTES, STIRRING TO PREVENT GARLIC BURNING.
ADD
3 T lemon juice
1/4 C water
COVER AND SIMMER 45 MINUTES
REMOVE COVER, RAISE HEAT, AND REDUCE LIQUID UNTIL SAUCE THICKENS AND COATS CHICKEN, STIRRING CONSTANTLY.

## HOT AND SPICY CHICKEN

MARINATE FOR 15 MINUTES OR MORE

1.5 kg (3 lb) frying chicken meat, cut into bite size pieces

IN A MIXTURE OF

2 tsp fresh ginger, shredded
1 T sherry, or wine vinegar
2 T soy sauce

IN A SMALL BOWL MIX

1 tsp star anise, or Sichuan peppercorns, ground
1/2 C chicken broth, or water
1 T soy sauce
2 T wine vinegar
1 T sugar
1/2 tsp sesame oil
1/2 tsp salt

AND SET ASIDE.

IN A LARGE POT HEAT

4 T peanut oil

AND ADD

1 scallion, shredded
2 dried red peppers, cut in 2.5 cm (1 inch) strips

FRY, STIRRING SEVERAL TIMES. ADD THE CHICKEN AND MARINADE. FRY, STIRRING, 1 TO 2 MINUTES. ADD THE STAR ANISE MIXTURE, MIX WELL, AND COOK OVER LOW HEAT UNTIL THE CHICKEN IS TENDER, ABOUT 10 TO 15 MINUTES.

ADD A MIXTURE OF

1 T corn starch
2 T water

COOK, STIRRING, UNTIL THICK.

## CREAMY GARLIC CHICKEN

DREDGE
8 chicken pieces, drumsticks and thighs
IN A MIXTURE OF
All purpose flour
Salt
Black pepper, ground
IN A LARGE POT HEAT
3 T vegetable oil
ADD THE CHICKEN AND BROWN. LOWER HEAT AND COOK 10 TO 15 MINUTES.
REMOVE CHICKEN AND RESERVE.
ADD TO THE POT, ON LOW HEAT
2 T olive oil
10 garlic cloves, crushed and chopped coarsely
STIR UNTIL GARLIC IS SOFT AND ADD
1/2 C dry white wine
BRING TO A BOIL, LOWER HEAT, AND SIMMER 2 TO 3 MINUTES.
RETURN CHICKEN TO THE POT AND ADD
1 1/2 C milk, heated
COVER AND SIMMER UNTIL CHICKEN IS DONE.
ADD A MIXTURE OF
1 T cornstarch
3 T milk
1/4 tsp red pepper powder
A LITTLE AT A TIME, AND STIR UNTIL SAUCE THICKENS.

## KAHLUA CHICKEN

SPRINKLE

4 chicken breasts, skinned

WITH

1/2 tsp onion salt

IN A FRYING PAN HEAT

1 T butter

ADD CHICKEN AND BROWN.

IN A BOWL COMBINE

1/3 C Kahlua

1/2 C orange juice

1 1/2 tsp lemon juice

1/2 T orange zest

POUR OVER CHICKEN, COVER AND SIMMER 35 TO 40 MINUTES. THICKEN THE SAUCE WITH A MIXTURE OF

2 T corn starch

2 T water

## ORANGE STAR ANISE CHICKEN

IN A SAUCEPAN COMBINE

3/4 C soy sauce
1 T brown sugar
1 T rice vinegar
Juice of one orange
2 inch piece dried tangerine, or mandarin orange, rind (optional)
1 whole star anise

BRING TO A BOIL AND ADD

1 T fresh ginger, grated
1 tsp red pepper powder
4 garlic cloves, chopped finely

SIMMER A FEW MINUTES AND ADD

2 tsp sesame oil

THICKEN WITH A MIXTURE OF

1 T water
1 T corn starch

AND POUR OVER

8 chicken pieces, skinned

MARINATE THE CHICKEN FOR 2 HOURS, TURNING OCASIONALLY. HEAT THE OVEN TO 400 F AND ROAST ON RACKS OVER COOKIE SHEETS, LINED WITH ALUMINUM FOIL, FOR 40 TO 45 MINUTES.

## GARLIC CHICKEN WITH CHILLIES

IN A LARGE FRYING PAN HEAT

3 T peanut oil

ADD AND BROWN, COOKING 15 MINUTES PER SIDE

1.5 kg (3 lb) frying chicken pieces, skinned

ADD BETWEEN THE CHICKEN PIECES

10 garlic cloves, chopped coarsely

3 dried red peppers, crumbled

FRY FOR 2 MINUTES AND ADD A MIXTURE OF

3/4 C vinegar

1/4 C soy sauce

3 T honey

COOK UNTIL CHICKEN IS DONE AND THE SAUCE REDUCES AND THICKENS. REMOVE CHICKEN AND RESERVE THE SAUCE.

SERVE WITH THE SAUCE AND RICE.

Here is an example of a recipe that was close to a disaster at first. I followed the original recipe exactly, and nobody liked it, including me. I thought the idea was sound so I started experimenting. This result was to my taste, and to the family's taste as well.

## MOROCCAN CHICKEN TAJINE

IN A LARGE FRYING PAN HEAT
3 T olive oil
ADD AND FRY UNTIL TRANSLUCENT
1 medium onion, grated or finely chopped
ADD
1/2 tsp cumin powder
1 tsp turmeric powder
1/2 tsp red pepper powder
1 tsp fresh ginger, grated
1/2 tsp cinnamon powder
1 tsp salt
1/2 tsp black pepper, ground
2 garlic cloves, chopped finely
STIR FRY UNTIL FRAGRANT AND ADD
2 C chicken stock, or water
BRING TO A BOIL, LOWER HEAT, AND ADD
1/4 C cilantro (fresh coriander leaves), chopped finely
1/4 C fresh parsley, chopped finely
STIR AND ADD
8 chicken pieces
SIMMER CHICKEN FOR 1 HOUR, TURNING OCCASIONALLY.
REMOVE CHICKEN, AND SET ASIDE
BRING SAUCE TO A BOIL AND ADD
1 1/2 tsp sugar
1 T lime, or lemon juice
BRING BACK TO A BOIL AND REDUCE SAUCE UNTIL THICK.
SERVE SAUCE WITH CHICKEN.

## CHICKEN CURRY

IN A LARGE SKILLET HEAT

3 T vegetable oil

ADD

500 g (1 lb) chicken meat, cubed

FRY UNTIL WHITE AND SOMEWHAT FIRM. TRANSFER TO A PLATE.

IN THE FRYING PAN HEAT

2 T vegetable oil

AND ADD

1 1/2 C onion, finely chopped

AND FRY UNTIL GOLDEN BROWN.

REDUCE HEAT AND ADD

1/4 tsp fennel seed, ground (optional)
1 tsp cumin powder
1 tsp coriander powder
1 tsp turmeric powder
1 tsp red pepper powder
1 T water

STIR CONSTANTLY, FRYING FOR ONE MINUTE.

STIR IN

1 C tomatoes, finely chopped
2 T cilantro (fresh coriander leaves) chopped, or parsley
1/2 C plain yogurt
1/2 C water
1 tsp salt
1 tsp garam masala

MIX THOROUGHLY. RETURN THE CHICKEN TO THE FRYING PAN, AND SIMMER 20 MINUTES.

BEST MADE AHEAD AND PUT IN FRIDGE OVERNIGHT.

REHEAT AND SERVE.

## COCONUT CHICKEN CURRY

WASH AND DRY

1.5 kg (3 lb) chicken pieces, skinned

SIMMER FOR 50 MINUTES IN A MIXTURE OF

2 400 ml (14 oz) Cans coconut milk, thick if you can get it

10 curry leaves

REMOVE AND DRAIN THE CHICKEN, RESERVING THE MILK.

IN A FRYING PAN HEAT

1 T ghee, or vegetable oil

ADD AND BROWN

2 onions, cut in medium size pieces

ADD

5 garlic cloves, chopped

FRY TWO MINUTES AND ADD THE CHICKEN. FRY UNTIL THE OIL SEPARATES.

ADD

1 T turmeric powder

2 tsp cumin powder

1 tsp coriander seed, crushed

FRY FOR 2 MINUTES.

ADD ONE THIRD OF THE COCONUT MILK AND

2 T lime juice

4 fresh red chillies, shredded

1 tsp fenugreek seed, ground

STIR TO COAT THE CHICKEN AND ADD THE REMAINING COCONUT MILK. SIMMER UNTIL CHICKEN IS WELL DONE.

SERVE SPRINKLED WITH

1 T sesame seeds, roasted

1 tsp black pepper, freshly ground

## COLUMBIAN CHICKEN BRAISED IN COCONUT MILK

IN A LARGE POT HEAT

2 T vegetable oil

ADD AND FRY UNTIL BROWN ON ALL SIDES

1 chicken, or rabbit, cut into serving pieces

REMOVE TO A BOWL AND RESERVE.

TO THE POT ADD

1 large onion, coarsely chopped

4 fresh red chilli peppers, shredded

6 garlic cloves, finely chopped

FRY UNTIL ONION IS GOLDEN AND ADD

1 C chicken stock

BRING TO A BOIL AND ADD

1/4 C lemon juice

3/4 C coconut milk

1/2 tsp dried rosemary, crushed

MIX AND RETURN THE RABBIT TO THE POT. RETURN TO A BOIL, REDUCE HEAT, AND SIMMER UNTIL RABBIT IS DONE, ABOUT 40 MINUTES. REMOVE RABBIT AND KEEP WARM.

TO THE STOCK ADD

1/2 C coconut milk

BRING TO A BOIL AND REDUCE LIQUID UNTIL THICK.

SERVE THE SAUCE WITH THE CHICKEN.

This is a recipe where I misinterpreted an ingredient that was asked for. The recipe called for anise Pepper, which I thought would be star anise. Well, it wasn't. I later discovered that the correct ingredient was Sichuan pepper. I tried the recipe with the Sichuan pepper and decided that it was better with the star anise. This was the mistake that lead to my doing research on the different names for ingredients.

## FRAGRENT CRISPY CHICKEN

SKIN
1kg (2 lb) chicken, thighs and drumsticks
AND MARINATE FOR SEVERAL HOURS IN A MIXTURE OF
1 tsp star anise, or Sichuan peppercorns, ground
1 T sherry, or Chinese rice wine
2 T honey
4 T soy sauce
3 tsp sesame oil
2 T lemon juice
1 T fresh ginger, grated
DREDGE THE CHICKEN IN
1/3 C corn starch, or more if needed
SET LEGS ASIDE UNTIL MARINADE SOAKS INTO CORNSTARCH. DEEP FRY IN VEGETABLE OIL UNTIL GOLDEN BROWN AND CRISPY.

## CRUNCHY CHICKEN WITH OREGANO

PREPARE

8 chicken pieces

RINSE, PAT DRY, AND SEASON WITH

Salt

Black pepper, ground

AND DREDGE IN

All purpose flour

DIP EACH PIECE IN A MIXTURE OF

2 eggs, slightly beaten

2 tsp water

ROLL THE CHICKEN IN A MIXTURE OF

1 C soda crackers, crushed

1 tsp dried oregano

PLACE IN A BAKING DISH AND BAKE AT 190 C (375 F) FOR 30 TO 40 MINUTES. 10 MINUTES BEFORE THE CHICKEN IS DONE MIX

3 T olive oil

2 T lemon juice

AND BRUSH OVER THE CHICKEN.

The next three recipes are a great cheap substitute for the commercial examples. The oil in the recipes ensures a crispy result.

## SHAKE AND BAKE CHICKEN

SKIN
1.5 kg (3 pounds) chicken drumsticks and thighs
IN A BOWL MIX
1/2 C fine bread crumbs
2 T oat bran (optional)
1 tsp dried oregano
1/2 tsp salt
1/2 tsp dried basil
1/2 tsp garlic powder
1/4 tsp red pepper powder
MIX WELL AND ADD
1 T vegetable oil
MIX WELL BY HAND AND PUT IN A GOOD PLASTIC BAG. SHAKE CHICKEN PIECES, ONE AT A TIME TO COAT. PLACE CHICKEN THICK SIDE UP ON A RACK IN A BAKING PAN. PRESS SOME OF THE LEFT OVER CRUMB MIXTURE, IF ANY, ONTO THE CHICKEN PIECES.
BAKE AT 205 C (400 F) FOR 45 MINUTES.

VARIATION

REPLACE OREGANO AND BASIL WITH
2 tsp poultry seasoning

## SOUTHERN SHAKE AND BAKE CHICKEN

IN A BOWL MIX

1/2 C fine bread crumbs
2 T oat bran (optional)
2 tsp dry mustard powder
1/2 tsp salt
1/2 tsp garlic powder
1/2 tsp curry powder
1/4 tsp cumin powder
1/2 tsp dried oregano
1/4 tsp paprika powder
1/2 tsp red pepper powder
1/2 tsp black pepper, ground

MIX WELL AND ADD

1 T vegetable oil

MIX WELL BY HAND AND PUT IN A GOOD PLASTIC BAG. SHAKE CHICKEN PIECES, ONE AT A TIME TO COAT. PLACE CHICKEN THICK SIDE UP ON A RACK IN A BAKING PAN. PRESS SOME OF THE LEFT OVER CRUMB MIXTURE, IF ANY, ONTO THE CHICKEN PIECES.
BAKE AT 205 C (400 F) FOR 45 MINUTES.

## CURRY SHAKE AND BAKE CHICKEN

IN A BOWL MIX

1/2 C  fine bread crumbs
3 T  oat bran (optional)
1/2 tsp  salt
1/2 tsp  garlic powder
1 tsp  curry powder
1/2 tsp  coriander powder
1/2 tsp  cumin powder
1 tsp  red pepper powder
1/2 tsp  garam masala

MIX WELL AND ADD

1 T  vegetable oil

MIX WELL BY HAND AND PUT IN A GOOD PLASTIC BAG. SHAKE CHICKEN PIECES, ONE AT A TIME TO COAT. PLACE CHICKEN THICK SIDE UP ON A RACK IN A BAKING PAN. PRESS SOME OF THE LEFT OVER CRUMB MIXTURE, IF ANY, ONTO THE CHICKEN PIECES.

BAKE AT 205 C (400 F) FOR 45 MINUTES.

## OVEN BARBECUED CHICKEN

(180 C (350 F) - 45 TO 60 minutes)

IN A SAUCEPAN COMBINE

1/4 C water
1/4 C apple cider vinegar
3 T vegetable oil
1/2 C chilli sauce, or ketchup and 1/4 tsp red pepper powder
3 T Worcestershire sauce
1 tsp dry mustard
1/2 tsp black pepper, ground
1 1/2 tsp salt
2 T onion, chopped

BRIING TO A BOIL, LOWER HEAT, AND SIMMER 5 TO 10 MINUTES.

INTO A LARGE BAKING DISH PLACE

1 chicken, cut up

POUR HALF OF THE SAUCE OVER THE CHICKEN AND BAKE AS ABOVE, UNCOVERED.

BASTE WITH THE REMAINING SAUCE EVERY 15 MINUTES.

This is my favorite Indian recipe. Served with Coconut Rice (page 185) and a complimentary vegetable.

## TANDOORI CHICKEN

IN A LARGE BOWL COMBINE

4 tsp red pepper powder, less if desired
1 small onion, chopped
5 garlic cloves, chopped finely
1 T fresh ginger, grated
1 tsp coriander powder
1/2 tsp cumin powder
1/2 tsp turmeric powder

ADD

1/2 C lime juice
1 C plain yogurt

MIX WELL.

SKIN AND MAKE DEEP GASHES IN

1.5 kg (3 lb) frying chicken pieces, skinned

ADD THE CHICKEN TO THE BOWL AND STUFF THE GASHES WITH THE ABOVE MIXTURE AND SPOON THE REMAINING MIXTURE OVER THE CHICKEN. MARINATE 2 HOURS. PLACE THE CHICKEN PIECES ON RACKS OVER BAKING PANS AND BAKE 40 TO 45 MINUTES AT 205 C (400 F). THE HOTTER AND QUICKER THIS DISH COOKS THE BETTER.

# FOIL BARBECUED CHICKEN

IN A SAUCEPAN COMBINE

2/3 C ketchup
1/3 C wine vinegar
2 tsp prepared mustard
1 tsp sweet paprika
2 T butter, melted
1 T Worcestershire sauce
2 garlic cloves, crushed
1/2 tsp dried oregano
1/2 tsp red pepper powder
1/4 tsp sugar
1 tsp salt

BRING TO A BOIL AND REMOVE FROM HEAT.
LINE A BAKING DISH WITH BUTTERED FOIL, AND ON IT ARRANGE

8 frying chicken pieces

ON TOP OF CHICKEN ARRANGE

1 C onion, sliced

POUR SAUCE OVER THE CHICKEN AND COVER WITH FOIL.
BAKE AT 190 C (375 F) FOR 40 MINUTES, REMOVE TOP FOIL AND BAKE ANOTHER 10 MINUTES.

## ROSEMARY ROAST CHICKEN

MAKE A MIXTURE OF

2 T olive oil
2 T garlic, chopped finely
1 T black pepper, coarsely ground
2 T lemon juice
1 T fresh rosemary, finely chopped
1 tsp dried oregano, preferably Greek

TUCK SOME OF THE MIXTURE UNDER THE BREAST SKIN OF

1 roasting chicken

USE THE REMAINING MIXTURE TO COAT, OR TUCK UNDER THE SKIN OF THE CHICKEN.

ROAST AT 180 C (350 F) FOR 50 MINUTES, OR UNTIL THE CHICKEN IS DONE.

This is a tasty departure from your standard roast chicken. It is one of the few roasting recipes found in Chinese cuisine. The classic procedure was to coat the leaf wrapped chicken in clay. Aluminum foil works very well.

## BEGGAR'S CHICKEN

MAKE A MARINADE OF

1/2 C dry sherry, or Chinese rice wine, or white wine
1/2 C soy sauce
1/4 C sesame oil
1/4 C sugar
1 T fresh ginger, chopped finely
2 scallions, chopped, or shallots.

MIX WELL AND PUT MARINADE IN A GOOD PLASTIC BAG, WITHOUT HOLES. INTO THE BAG PUT

1 chicken, about 2 kg (4 pounds)

SLOSH AROUND, PUSH OUT MOST OF THE AIR, SEAL, AND PUT IT IN A BOWL. MARINATE OVER NIGHT, TURNING OCCASIONALLY, IN A FRIDGE. MAKE A STUFFING USING THE STUFFED LOTUS LEAF PARCEL RECIPE (page 181) AND RESERVE.

WHEN READY TO ROAST THE CHICKEN, STEAM UNTIL PLIABLE

2 lotus leaves

TO WRAP CHICKEN, PUT A LEAF ON A LARGE SHEET OF Aluminum foil, large enough to wrap chicken

PLACE THE CHICKEN, DRAINED, RESERVING THE MARINADE, ON THE LEAF. STUFF THE CHICKEN WITH THE RICE MIXTURE. WRAP THE TOP OF THE CHICKEN WITH THE OTHER LEAF AND ENCLOSE WITH FOIL. ROAST IN AN OVEN AT 180 C (350 F) UNTIL CHICKEN IS WELL DONE, ABOUT 3 TO 4 HOURS. WRAP LEFTOVER STUFFING IN LOTUS LEAF, AS IN THE LOTUS LEAF PARCEL RECIPE IF DESIRED. STEAM THE PARCELS STARTING ABOUT 45 TO 50 MINUTES BEFORE CHICKEN IS DONE.

BRING THE RESERVED MARINADE TO A BOIL IN A SAUCEPAN AND THICKEN WITH

1 T  corn starch
1 T  water
SERVE SAUCE WITH CHICKEN.
SEE VARIATION BELOW.

BEGGAR'S CHICKEN VARIATION (quick method)

CUT UP THE CHICKEN. MARINATE THE CHICKEN FOR TWO HOURS. STEAM OR BOIL LOTUS LEAVES UNTIL PLIABLE AND KEEP BETWEEN LAYERS OF A WET TOWEL. WHEN READY, WRAP ONE OR TWO PIECES OF CHICKEN IN LOTUS LEAF AND FOIL. BAKE FOR 1 HOUR AT 400 F.

## ORANGE ROAST DUCK

(preheat oven to180 C (350 F))

IN A LARGE POT BOIL FOR 2 MINUTES AND DRAIN
1  duck
IN A BOWL MIX
3/4 C  orange juice
1/4 C  honey
1/4 C  soy sauce
1 tsp  fresh ginger, grated
1 tsp  garlic, chopped finely
ROAST DUCK FOR 2 HOURS, BASTING EVERY 20 MINUTES WITH THE ORANGE MIXTURE.

I have never tasted a better roast duck recipe. This has been modified significantly from the original. If you care to try it in the original manner baste the duck while it cooks. However, be careful doing this as you may end up, as I did, with a charred black duck. Preparing the sauce and serving it separately also allows you to slather it liberally on any piece of your duck meat. Yes it is that good.

## SICHUAN PEPPER ROAST DUCK

WASH AND DRY

1 duck

RUB INSIDE AND OUT WITH A MIXTURE

1 T Sichuan peppercorns, ground coarsely
1 tsp salt

HEAT OVEN TO 230 C (450 F). ROAST FOR 10 MINUTES.
REDUCE HEAT TO 165 C (325 F) AND ROAST FOR 2 HOURS, OR UNTIL DUCK IS DONE.
MEANWHILE, TO THE TOP HALF OF A DOUBLE BOILER ADD

1 C honey
1 C brown sugar
1/2 T Sichuan peppercorns, ground coarsely
4 garlic cloves, finely chopped
1 T fresh ginger, grated
1/4 C soy sauce

BRING TO A BOIL, STIRRING CONSTANTLY, UNTIL A CANDY THERMOMETER READS 113 C (235 F).
REMOVE FROM HEAT AND KEEP WARM ON THE DOUBLE BOILER. THE SAUCE BECOMES VERY THICK IF YOU LET IT COOL TOO MUCH.
SERVE THE DUCK WITH THE SAUCE.

## DUCK WITH TOMATO RHUBARB SAUCE

ROAST

1 duck

AT 220 C (425 F) FOR 30 MINUTES AND THEN REDUCE TO 165 C (325 F). ROAST ANOTHER 1 1/2 HOURS, OR UNTIL DUCK IS DONE.

MEANWHILE, COMBINE

500 g (1 lb) tomatoes, chopped coarsely
1 large stalk rhubarb, cut in 2.5 cm (1 inch) pieces
2 T sugar
2 T cider vinegar
1 T fresh ginger, grated

BRING TO A BOIL AND SIMMER, STIRRING OCCASIONALLY, FOR 1 HOUR. SERVE WITH THE DUCK.

Here we have a good example of Persian cuisine.

## DUCK IN POMEGRANATE NUT SAUCE

IN A LARGE POT HEAT
3 T vegetable oil
BROWN
1 duck, cut in serving pieces
REMOVE PIECES AND RESERVE. IN THE SAME OIL FRY
1 medium onion, coarsely chopped
UNTIL BROWN, STIRRING OCCASIONALLY, AND ADD
2/3 C walnuts, chopped or pounded
COOK, STIRRING, FOR ABOUT 2 MINUTES AND ADD
1 C pomegranate juice (see note below)
4 T lemon juice
2 T sugar (add more after cooking to taste)
1/2 C water
1/2 tsp salt
1/4 tsp nutmeg, grated
1/4 tsp cinnamon powder
1/4 tsp black pepper, ground
BRING TO A SIMMER, STIR, AND ADD THE DUCK. COOK GENTLY FOR 1 1/2 HOURS, OR UNTIL DUCK IS TENDER, TURNING WHEN ABOUT HALF COOKED. REMOVE THE DUCK AND POUR THE SAUCE INTO A BOWL. ALLOW THE SAUCE TO SETTLE AND SKIM OFF THE FAT. THIN THE SAUCE WITH A LITTLE WATER IF NECESSARY.

NOTE

TO USE FRESH POMEGRANATES PEEL AND REMOVE THE FLESHY SEEDS, DISCARDING THE PITH. PUT THE FLESH IN A FOOD PROCESSOR AND BLEND A FEW SECONDS TO BREAK THE MEMBRANES. STRAIN THE JUICE INTO A BOWL, SQUEEZING TO REMOVE AS MUCH AS POSSIBLE.

## WALNUT APPLE STUFFING FOR CHICKEN

IN A FRYING PAN HEAT

2 T vegetable oil

ADD

1 C walnuts, coarsely chopped
1/2 C onion, chopped
1/2 C celery, chopped

FRY UNTIL ONION IS TENDER.
REMOVE FROM HEAT AND ADD

4 C bread crumbs
2 C tart apples, peeled and chopped
1/4 C fresh parsley, chopped

MOISTEN TO TASTE WITH

Apple cider or juice

MIX WELL, AND SEASON WITH

Salt
Black pepper, ground

REFRIGERATE UNTIL READY TO STUFF THE CHICKEN.

## FRUIT WILD RICE STUFFING

SIMMER UNTIL SOFTENED
1/2 C port wine
1 C dried fruit
AND RESERVE
INTO A POT PUT
1/2 C wild rice
1 C brown rice
5 1/2 C water
1 1/2 tsp salt
BRING TO A BOIL AND REDUCE HEAT. COOK FOR 1 HOUR.
DRAIN AND RESERVE RICE.
INTO A FRYING PAN PUT
2 C apples, chopped
1 C celery, chopped finely
1/2 C onion, chopped finely
1/3 C margarine
MIX AND FRY UNTIL SOFT
MIX TOGETHER THE FRUIT, RICE, AND APPLE MIXTURES.

## OLD FASHIONED SAGE TURKEY STUFFING

IN A SAUCEPAN HEAT

1/4 C butter

ADD AND FRY UNTIL SOFT

2 medium onions, finely chopped

1 C celery, chopped

REMOVE FROM HEAT AND COMBINE IN A BOWL WITH

10 C bread, cubed and dried

1 tsp salt

1/8 tsp black pepper, ground

1/4 C chicken stock

3/4 tsp dried sage

1 T parsley flakes

VARIATION (APPLE RAISIN STUFFING)

PREPARE SAGE STUFFING BUT OMIT THE LAST THREE INGREDIENTS WITH.

1 C raisins

1 medium apple, cored and chopped

1/2 tsp cinnamon powder

1/4 tsp nutmeg, grated

## CHILLI STUFFING FOR TURKEY

IN A POT HEAT

3 T butter

ADD

1 large onion, coarsely chopped
5 garlic cloves, chopped finely
5 fresh green chillies, chopped finely

FRY UNTIL SOFT AND ADD

125 g (1/4 lb) ground veal or pork

FRY 5 MINUTES AND TRANSFER TO A BOWL.

ADD

125 g (1/4 lb) white bread crumbs
1/3 C dry white wine, or chicken stock
3 T fresh parsley, finely chopped
1/4 C pine nuts, or walnuts, chopped
1/8 tsp cloves, ground
1/4 tsp black pepper, ground
1/2 tsp dried thyme
1/2 tsp salt

MIX WELL AND STUFF A TURKEY.

# FISH AND SEAFOOD

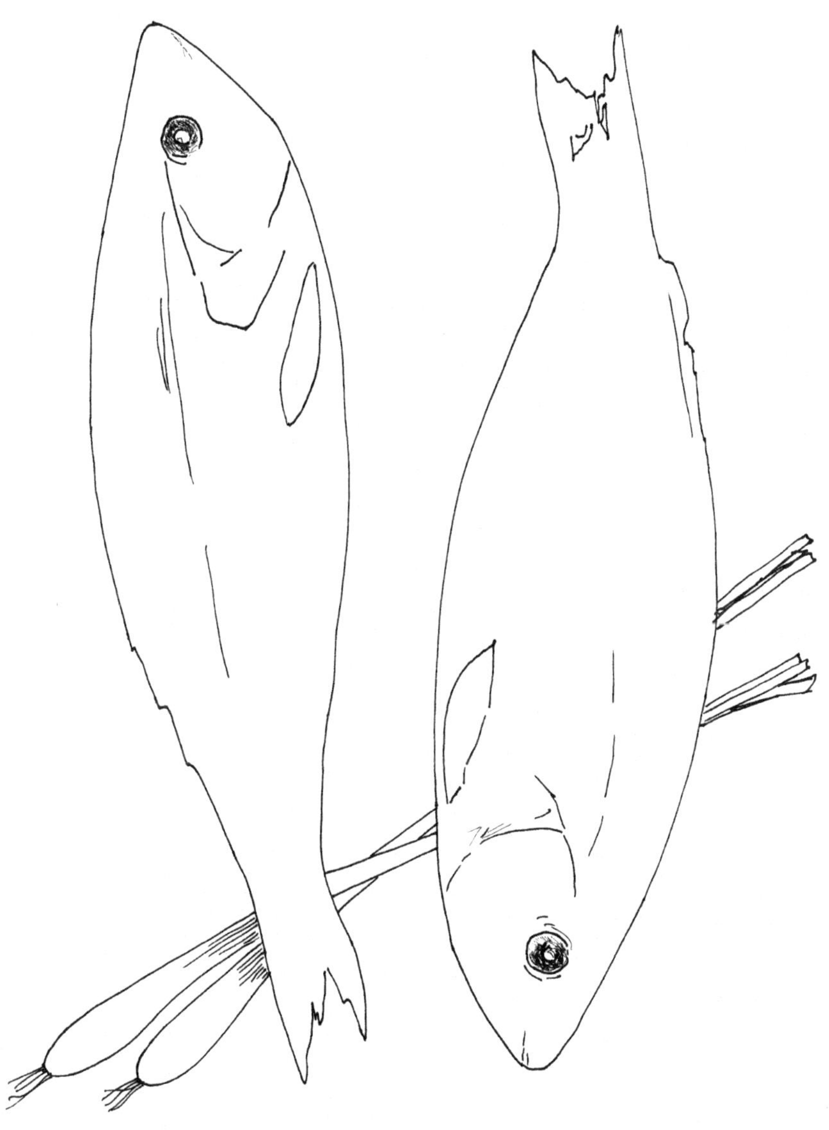

This is my favorite way to prepare salmon.

## TERIAKI SALMON

FILLET AND CUT INTO 3 INCH PIECES

1 salmon

MAKE A MARINADE OF

1 C soy sauce

4 T lemon juice

2 T honey

2 garlic cloves, chopped finely

1 T fresh ginger, grated

PUT THE SALMON IN A FLAT DISH AND POUR THE MARINADE OVER. MARINATE FOR A FEW HOURS, TURNING OCASIONALLY, OR OVERNIGHT IN A FRIDGE

GRILL ON A BARBECUE OR IN AN OVEN.

This is quick and easy.

## SALMON STEAKS WITH OREGANO AND LEMON

IN A BOWL MIX

1/4 C all purpose flour

1 1/2 tsp dried oregano

COAT

4 salmon steaks

WITH THE MIXTURE. PLACE THE SALMON IN A FRYING PAN AND DRIZZLE

Lemon juice

LIBERALLY OVER THE STEAKS. COOK A FEW MINUTES AND CAREFULLY TURN THE STEAKS OVER. DRIZZLE MORE LEMON JUICE ON TOP AND COOK UNTIL DONE.

This was my first try with fermented black beans with fish and I have never looked back.

## STEAMED SALMON WITH BLACK BEAN SAUCE

IN A SAUCEPAN MIX

2 tsp sesame oil
2 T fermented black beans, rinsed and coarsely chopped
1 1/2 T garlic, chopped
1 T fresh ginger, grated
3 T scallion, chopped
3 T soy sauce
2/3 C water

BRING TO A BOIL, REDUCE HEAT, AND SIMMER 1 MINUTE.
ADD A MIXTURE OF

1 tsp corn starch
1 tsp water

BRING THE MIXTURE TO A BOIL, STIR UNTIL THICKENED, AND REMOVE FROM HEAT.
RUB

500 g (1 lb) salmon fillets

WITH A MIXTURE OF

1 tsp salt
2 tsp sesame oil

PLACE THE SALMON ON A PLATE, SUSPENDED ON A RACK, IN A STEAMER, AND STEAM FOR 6 MINUTES.
SERVE THE SALMON WITH THE SAUCE.

## DILLED FILLETS

ON A BROILER PAN, WITH THICK PART UP, ARRANGE

4 sole fillets, (salmon or sea bass can be substituted)

BRUSH WITH

1 1/2 tsp lemon juice

SPRINKLE WITH

4 garlic cloves, chopped finely

2 T dried dill weed

BROIL 5 MINUTES, OR UNTIL DONE.

FOR THE SAUCE COMBINE

1/2 C plain yogurt

1/2 C cucumber, finely chopped

1 T scallion, or chives, chopped

Black pepper, ground

SERVE WITH THE FISH.

## BAKED SALMON WITH LEMON AND DILL

SPRINKLE THE INSIDE OF
1 salmon, whole, dressed
WITH
Dried dill
THINLY SLICE
2 lemons
AND PLACE HALF THE SLICES IN THE BODY CAVITY.
CLOSE THE SALMON AND PLACE IT ON IT'S SIDE ON
Aluminum foil, enough to enclose salmon
PUT REMAINING LEMON SLICES ON TOP OF THE SALMON AND SPRINKLE WITH
Dried dill
SEAL THE FOIL AND PLACE THE SALMON IN A ROASTING PAN.
BAKE AT 220 C (425 F), 15 MINUTES PER INCH OF THICKNESS UNTIL DONE.

## BACON BROILED TROUT

RUB, INSIDE AND OUT
1 trout, whole, dressed
WITH
1 lemon, cut in two
SPRINKLE THE INSIDE OF THE TROUT WITH
Black pepper, ground
WRAP TROUT, TO COVER, WITH
Bacon slices
AND SECURE WITH TOOTHPICKS. PLACE ON A BARBECUE, OR GRILL IN AN OVEN, FOR 4-8 MINUTES, TURNING ONCE.

Another wonderful Chinese inspired favorite.

## FIVE SPICE TILAPIA FILLETS

FOR THE SAUCE, COMBINE IN A BOWL

2 T scallion, thinly sliced
2 T orange juice
1 T lemon juice
1 T soy sauce
1 tsp brown sugar
2 tsp vinegar
1 tsp fresh ginger, grated

AND SET ASIDE.

MAKE A MIXTURE OF

1/2 tsp five spice powder
1/4 tsp salt
1/4 tsp red pepper powder

AND SPRINKLE ON BOTH SIDES OF

4 tilapia filets, or other white fish

IN A LARGE SKILLET, ON MEDIUM HIGH, HEAT

1 T vegetable oil

ADD THE FILETS AND COOK 2 MINUTES ON EACH SIDE, OR UNTIL FISH FLAKES WHEN TESTED WITH A FORK.

SERVE WITH THE SAUCE.

This recipe should be done outside, or in a well ventilated area. The process creates a great deal of smoke.

## BLACKENED FISH

FILLET AND RESERVE

1.5 kg (3 lb) red snapper, or salmon, enough for 6 people

FOR THE SEASONING, MIX AND GRIND AS FINELY AS POSSIBLE

1 T paprika, powder
2 tsp salt
1 tsp onion powder
1 tsp garlic powder
1 tsp red pepper powder
1 tsp black pepper, ground
1/2 tsp dried thyme

DIP THE FILLETS IN

4 T butter, melted

PLACE FILLETS ON A WARM PLATE AND SPRINKLE WITH SOME OF THE SEASONING MIXTURE. TURN OVER AND SPRINKLE THE OTHER SIDE.

HEAT A CAST IRON FRYING PAN, (DO NOT ADD OIL), UNTIL IT SMOKES. PLACE A FILLET IN FRYING PAN AND SPOON

1 tsp butter, melted

OVER THE FILLET.

COOK AT HIGHEST HEAT FOR 2 MINUTES. TURN AND SPOON SOME BUTTER OVER THE FILLET. WHEN THE SECOND SIDE IS DONE REMOVE FILLET AND COOK ANOTHER, REPEATING THE PROCESS.

## HUNAN STEAMED FISH

SOAK
6 dried black mushrooms
FOR 25 MINUTES. PRESS OUT MOISTURE, SHRED, DISCARDING STEMS, AND RESERVE.
CLEAN
1 whole, 1 kg (2 lb), carp, cod, or salmon
DRY WELL AND SCORE SKIN LIGHTLY, MAKING CUTS 2.5 cm (1 inch) APART AND SET ASIDE.
MIX TOGETHER
1 T sherry, or rice wine
1/2 tsp salt
RUB OVER INSIDE AND OUTSIDE OF THE FISH. PLACE THE FISH ON A DISH THAT WILL FIT IN A STEAMER SO THAT THE STEAM WILL CIRCULATE WELL.
IN A BOWL MIX
2 T bacon, chopped finely
1 T fermented black beans, rinsed and chopped coarsely
1/2 tsp red pepper powder
1 T garlic, chopped finely
2 T sesame oil
2 scallions, including tops, cut in 5 cm (2 inch) pieces and cut lengthwise
1 T fresh ginger, grated
2 T soy sauce
1/4 tsp salt
PLACE MIXTURE ON THE FISH AND PLACE DISH IN THE STEAMER. COVER TIGHTLY AND STEAM FOR 10 TO 15 MINUTES, BEING SURE TO NOT OVERCOOK FISH. SERVE IMMEDIATELY.

## HUNAN STEAMED FISH VARIATION 1 (microwave)

USING FISH FILLETS, OMIT RUB AND PRECOOK THE SAUCE, ADDING
1 Can straw mushrooms, drained
PLACE FILLETS IN A BAKING DISH AND POUR SAUCE OVER

THE FISH. MICROWAVE UNTIL THE FISH IS DONE.

HUNAN STEAMED FISH VARIATION 2

HEAT
1 T vegetable oil
2 tsp sesame oil
ADD
3/4 C chives, chopped finely
1 T ginger, grated
4 garlic cloves, chopped finely
5 dried black mushrooms, soaked 25 minutes and chopped, discarding stems
AND FRY UNTIL GARLIC IS BROWNED.
ADD
1 Can straw mushrooms, drained
HEAT THROUGH AND ADD
2 T fermented black beans, rinsed and chopped coarsely
2 T soy sauce
HEAT THOROUGHLY TO BLEND. SERVE WITH VIRTUALLY ANY FISH.

## SEAFOOD CURRY

IN A DOUBLE BOILER POT HEAT
1/2 C butter
ADD
1 C onion, chopped
FRY UNTIL TRANSLUCENT AND MIX IN
1/2 C all purpose flour
1 tsp salt
1 T curry powder
GRADUALLY STIR IN
3 C milk
PLACE THE POT ON THE DOUBLE BOILER BOTTOM AND COOK UNTIL THICK AND SMOOTH, STIRRING CONSTANTLY.
ADD, AND MIX IN
6 T ketchup
3 C seafood, (cod, shrimp, or mussels, or a mixture)
SIMMER 10 MINUTES, AND SERVE.

## CURRY FRIED COD

COAT
1 kg (2 lb) cod, cut in 5 cm (2 inch) strips
IN A MIXTURE OF
3/4 C all purpose flour
1/4 C curry powder
IN A FRYING PAN HEAT
2 T vegetable oil
BROWN FISH ON BOTH SIDES, UNTIL DONE, AND SPRINKLE WITH PARSLEY.

## COCONUT FISH CURRY

HEAT
2 T  vegetable oil
IN A HEAVY SKILLET AND ADD
1  cinnamon stick (about one inch)
2  green cardamom pods
FRY BRIEFLY AND ADD
1 T  garlic, sliced
1 T  fresh ginger, juliened
4  fresh green chillies, slit open
1  medium onion, sliced
FRY UNTIL THE ONIONS BECOME TRANSLUCENT.
ADD
500 g (1 lb)  fish fillets
1  tomato, chopped
1 tsp  turmeric powder
1 C  water
1/2 tsp  black peppercorns, crushed
1 T  lime juice
4  curry leaves
1/2 tsp  salt
AND MIX GENTLY.  COOK, COVERED, ON LOW, FOR 10 MINUTES, OR UNTIL FISH IS TENDER.
ADD
2 C  coconut milk
SIMMER FOR 2 MINUTES.
GARNISH WITH
Fried tomato slices

## SHRIMP OR PRAWN CURRY

IN A FRYING PAN FRY UNTIL GOLDEN BROWN

1/2 C onion, chopped

ADD

3 medium tomatoes, blended

AND COOK OVER MEDIUM HEAT FOR 10 MINUTES.

ADD

2 tsp salt
2 tsp garlic, chopped finely
1 1/2 tsp fresh ginger, grated
1/3 tsp red pepper powder
2 tsp coriander powder
2 tsp cumin powder
1/3 tsp turmeric powder

COOK 2-3 MINUTES AND ADD

1/2 C tomato paste

COOK 2 TO 3 MINUTES AND LOWER HEAT TO JUST KEEP WARM.

IN A FRYING PAN HEAT

1/3 C vegetable oil, or ghee

AND ADD

3/4 cinnamon stick
1 tsp cloves, ground
4 coriander seeds, crushed, or 1/8 tsp powder
1 T cilantro (fresh coriander leaves), or Parsley

COOK A FEW MINUTES AND STRAIN OIL INTO THE ABOVE SAUCE. BRING THE SAUCE TO A SIMMER AND ADD

750 g (1 1/2 lb) prawns (jumbo shrimp)

SIMMER 5 MINUTES AND SERVE.

## MEXICAN BROILED GARLIC PRAWNS

IN A SAUCEPAN HEAT
5 T butter
AND ADD
3 garlic cloves, finely chopped
1 tsp red pepper powder
1 T lime or lemon juice
SIMMER 1 MINUTE.
PLACE
1 lb prawns (jumbo shrimp)
ON SKEWERS AND BASTE WITH THE BUTTER MIXTURE. BROIL, TURNING ONCE, UNTIL JUST PINK, ABOUT 3 MINUTES.

## PRAWN BROIL

WRAP
6 prawns (jumbo shrimps)
AROUND
6 pineapple segments
WRAP A PIECE OF
3 bacon strips, cut in half
AROUND EACH PRAWN. SECURE WITH TOOTHPICKS AND BROIL UNTIL BACON IS CRISP. SERVE HOT.

An easy way to get the same effect of an old classic.

## IMPERIAL OYSTERS

(230 C (450 F) - 15 to 18 minutes)

IN A BOWL COMBINE
125 g (1/4 lb) cooked crab meat, flaked
4 oz cream cheese
2 T mayonnaise
2 T onion, chopped finely
4 1/2 tsp medium dry sherry, or wine
2 tsp dry mustard
PLACE
12 oysters
EVENLY IN THE BOTTOM OF A BAKING DISH. SPREAD THE CRAB MIXTURE EVENLY OVER TOP AND BAKE AS ABOVE.
THE OYSTERS CAN ALSO BE DONE ON THE HALF SHELL.

## PAN-FRIED OYSTERS AND BACON

WRAP EACH OF
12 oysters
WITH A PIECE OF
3 bacon strips, cut in 4 pieces
DIP IN A MIXTURE OF
1 egg, beaten
1 T water
IN A FRYING PAN HEAT
1 T vegetable oil
AND GENTLY PLACE THE OYSTERS IN IT. BROWN ON BOTH SIDES.

## GREEK FRIED SQUID

CLEAN

1.5 kg (3 lb) squid

SLICE BODIES IN 1/4 INCH RINGS, AND REMOVING BEAKS FROM TENTACLES. DRY RINGS AND TENTACLES THOROUGHLY.

SPRINKLE WITH

Salt

ROLL IN

All purpose flour

IN A FRYING PAN HEAT

Olive Oil, 1.3 cm (1/2 inch) deep

FRY RINGS UNTIL GOLDEN BROWN. SERVE WITH

Parsley, chopped
Dried oregano, crumbled
Lemon wedges
Tzatziki sauce (page 64).

.

# PASTA POTATOES AND RICE

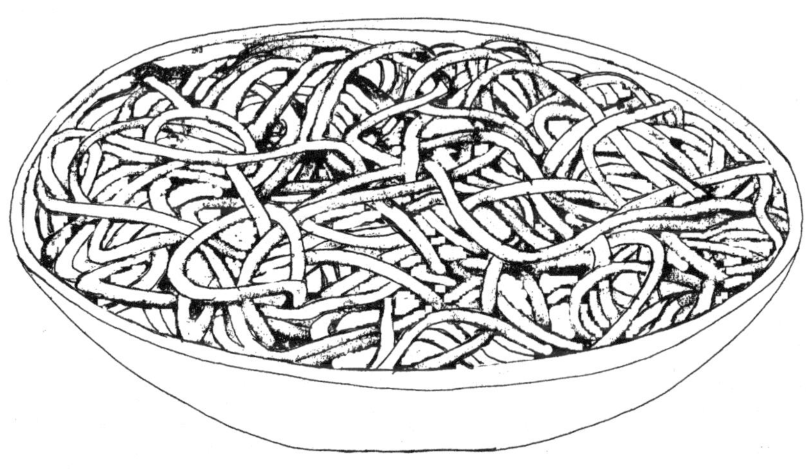

## LEMON POTATOES

PEEL AND CUT INTO 6 mm (1/4 INCH) SLICES

1 kg (2 lb) potatoes

DROP INTO BOILING WATER AND BOIL FOR 5 MINUTES, OR UNTIL BARELY TENDER. DRAIN THOROUGHLY.

INTO A FRYING PAN PUT

3 T olive oil

HEAT AND ADD ENOUGH POTATOES TO COVER THE BOTTOM. BROWN THE POTATOES ALL OVER AND THEN ADD SOME MORE. ADD MORE POTATOES AS THE SECOND BUNCH BEGINS TO BROWN, AND SO ON, UNTIL ALL THE POTATOES ARE ADDED AND WELL BROWNED, ADDING OIL AS NECESSARY.

ADD A MIXTURE OF

Zest of 1/2 lemon
3 garlic cloves, chopped finely
Large pinch nutmeg, grated
Salt
Black pepper, ground

TOSS THE POTATOES AND FRY THEM UNTIL THEY ARE CRUSTY. WHEN YOU ARE READY TO SERVE THE POTATOES REHEAT THEM IN THE PAN AND TOSS WITH A MIXTURE OF

1 T fresh basil, chopped finely
1 T fresh parsley, chopped finely
2 T butter
1 T lemon juice

SERVE AT ONCE

## BAKED POTATOES

PREHEAT OVEN TO 350 F AND BAKE FOR ONE HOUR

Medium potatoes

## GREEK POTATOES WITH LEMON SAUCE

PEEL

5 medium potatoes

PUT THEM INTO A POT AND ADD

Water, enough to cover

1 T salt

BOIL UNTIL THE POTATOES ARE ALMOST TENDER, ABOUT 15 TO 20 MINUTES. REMOVE THE POT FROM THE HEAT, LET STAND FOR 10 MINUTES, AND DRAIN.

IN A SMALL BOWL COMBINE

1/3 C olive oil

2 T fresh parsley, finely chopped

1 small onion, finely chopped

4 T lemons juice

1/2 tsp salt

PEEL AND SLICE THE POTATOES INTO A LARGE BOWL. ADD THE SAUCE AND TOSS WELL. SERVE HOT.

## OVEN FRIES

CUT INTO 1.3 cm (1/2 inch) STICKS OR SLICES

6 to 8 potatoes, depending on size, peeled or well cleaned

PUT IN A LEAKPROOF PLASTIC BAG AND ADD

4 T vegetable oil

HOLD BAG OPENING CLOSED TIGHTLY AND TUMBLE POTATOES TO COAT. POUR OUT ONTO A BAKING SHEET. BAKE AT 205 C (400 F) FOR 45 MINUTES, FOR SLICED POTATOES, AND 1 HOUR, OR MORE, FOR FRIES. TURN ONCE OR TWICE DURING COOKING.

These are so yummy.

## CANDIED SWEET POTATOES

(180 C (350 F) - 1 hour)

PEEL AND SLICE 6 mm (1/4 inch) THICK
1 large sweet potato, or yam
PLACE IN A BAKING DISH AND ON TOP ADD
2 T water
2 T butter, cut in chunks
2 T brown sugar
BAKE IN OVEN AS ABOVE.

## GARLIC MASHED POTATOES

INTO A POT PUT
6 medium potatoes, peeled and cubed
8 garlic cloves, peeled
Water, enough to cover
BOIL UNTIL POTATOES ARE TENDER AND DRAIN.
ADD
1 T butter
1/4 C milk
MASH AND SERVE.

## POTATO CAKES WITH GREEN CHILLIES

COOK IN BOILING WATER UNTIL PEEL CRACKS

500 g (1 lb) potatoes

SET ASIDE AND COOL.

IN A BOWL MIX

4 scallions chopped finely
1 tsp fresh ginger juice
2 T parsley, finely chopped
1 tsp salt
1 tsp garam masala
1 fresh green chilli, or more, chopped finely
1 T lemon juice
1 C peas cooked and slightly crushed

SET ASIDE. PEEL POTATOES AND MASH THEM WELL IN A BOWL. ADD THE REST OF THE INGREDIENTS AND MIX WELL.

FORM INTO PATTIES AND DIP IN

2 eggs, beaten

FRY UNTIL GOLDEN BROWN. SERVE WITH CHUTNEY. ALSO GOOD DIPPED IN PAKORA BATTER AND DEEP FRIED.

# PAELLA

IN A LARGE FRYING PAN, OR PAELLA PAN, HEAT

1/2 C olive oil

ADD AND BROWN

1 chicken, cut up

ADD

250 g (1/2 lb) pork, cubed

4 chorizo sausages, cut in 1.3 cm (1/2 inch) pieces

FRY 10 MINUTES, REMOVE ALL THE MEATS AND SET ASIDE.

TO THE FRYING PAN ADD

3 C rice

Pinch saffron, or paprika, for color

1 tsp salt

FRY UNTIL RICE TURNS A LIGHT GOLDEN COLOR AND ADD

1 onion, chopped

4 garlic cloves, chopped

FRY UNTIL ONION IS SOFT.

ADD, MEASURING HOW MANY CUPS THERE ARE

4 tomatoes, cut in small pieces

BRING TO A BOIL, REDUCE HEAT, AND SIMMER FOR 5 MINUTES.

ADD

Chicken stock, or water, (to add up to 6 Cups, including the measurement taken for the tomatoes).

1 C green peas

2 T fresh parsley, chopped

RETURN THE CHICKEN AND THE SAUSAGES TO THE PAN AND MIX ALL TOGETHER.

ON TOP ARRANGE

6 prawns (jumbo shrimp)

12 clams in their shell

BRING TO A BOIL, REDUCE HEAT AND SIMMER FOR 20 MINUTES. COVER AND LET STAND 20 MINUTES. DISCARD ANY UNOPENED CLAMS

This is an awesome combination, even though the preparation takes some time. The recipe I started with called for duck meat, but this is better. The parcels can be frozen, thawed, and steamed again to reheat.

## STUFFED LOTUS LEAF PARCELS

RINSE THREE TIMES AND DRAIN

1 1/2 C glutinous rice (sweet, sticky rice)

INTO A POT PUT

2 1/2 C water

AND ADD THE RICE. BRING TO A BOIL, LOWER HEAT, AND SIMMER UNTIL THE WATER IS ABSORBED, ABOUT 25 MINUTES.

HEAT A FRYING PAN AND ADD

1 1/2 T peanut oil
1/2 tsp salt
1 1/2 tsp fresh ginger, grated
1 1/2 tsp garlic, chopped finely
1 C cooked chicken cut into 6 mm (1/4 inch) cubes
1 C Chinese sausage, cut into 6 mm (1/4 inch) cubes
1/2 C roast pork, cut into 6 mm (1/4 inch) cubes
1 tsp honey
4 dried black mushrooms, soaked 25 minutes and cut into 6 mm (1/4 inch) cubes, discarding stems

MIX WELL AND COOK 1 MINUTE.

ADD AND STIR IN

4 T rice wine, or a dry white wine

REMOVE ALL FROM THE SKILLET AND PUT IN A LARGE MIXING BOWL.

TO THE BOWL ADD

4 water chestnuts, cut into 6 mm (1/4 inch) cubes
1/2 C scallions, or chives, or shallots, finely chopped
2 T oyster sauce (optional)
1 1/2 T peanut oil
1 1/2 tsp sesame oil
1 tsp sugar
2 tsp soy sauce

1 pinch black pepper, ground

MIX WELL. ADD THE PREPARED RICE AND MIX WELL. PREPARE

4 lotus leaves, steamed until flexible and cut in half

PLACE THE HALVES OF EACH LEAF ON TOP OF ONE ANOTHER SO THAT THERE ARE NO HOLES. DIVIDE THE RICE MIXTURE BETWEEN THE LEAVES. MOUND THE RICE IN THE CENTER AND FOLD TO MAKE A PARCEL. PLACE THE PACKAGE IN A STEAMER, FOLDED SIDE DOWN, AND STEAM 30 TO 40 MINUTES. YOU COULD ALTERNATIVELY MAKE TWO SMALL PACKETS WITH EACH LEAF.

## RICE PARMIGIANA

(350 F - 30 minutes)

IN A BAKING DISH MIX

2 C cooked rice
1 C parsley, chopped
1/2 C scallions, chopped
1 C parmesan cheese
3 eggs
1/4 C milk
Salt
Black pepper, ground

MIX WELL, BAKE AS ABOVE, AND SERVE.

Use your leftover rice for this.

## FRIED RICE WITH PORK OR CHICKEN

SOAK FOR 25 MINUTES
4 dried black mushrooms
DRAIN AND SQUEEZE OUT WATER. CHOP, DISCARDING STEMS AND SET ASIDE.
IN A LARGE POT HEAT
1 1/2 T vegetable oil
1 tsp sesame oil
TO THE POT ADD
2 medium onions, chopped
4 garlic cloves, finely chopped
1 T fresh ginger, grated
FRY UNTIL BROWNED AND ADD
3 bacon slices, with most fat removed, chopped
STIR FRY A MINUTE OR TWO. ADD THE MUSHROOMS AND
1 1/2 C cooked pork, cubed
FRY UNTIL HEATED THROUGH AND ADD
1 1/2 T soy sauce
1/2 tsp sugar
MIX WELL AND ADD
1 1/2 C peas, or corn niblets
MIX AND ADD
3 C cooked rice, the drier the better
MIX WELL AND FRY UNTIL FAIRLY DRY.
MOVE ALL TO THE EDGE OF THE POT, LEAVING A WELL IN THE CENTER.
ADD TO WELL
2 eggs, beaten
WHEN EGG BEGINS TO SET MIX ALL TOGETHER.
STIR UNTIL EGG IS COOKED AND ALL IS A BIT DRY.

# ORANGE RICE WITH ALMONDS AND PISTACIOS

ZEST

2 large seedless oranges

RESERVE THE ZEST. REMOVE THE ORANGE PEEL AND WHITE PARTS AND DISCARD. CHOP THE ORANGE AND PUT IT IN A BLENDER WITH

4 garlic cloves, chopped finely
1 T ginger, grated
1 T red pepper flakes
1 T curry powder
1/2 tsp cinnamon powder
1/2 tsp dried dill
1/4 C orange juice, frozen concentrate
3 T sugar
1/4 tsp fennel seeds

BLEND THE INGREDIENTS WELL.

IN A LARGE FRYING PAN, OR CASSEROLE, WITH A TIGHT FITTING LID, MELT

1/2 C butter

ADD AND FRY THE ORANGE ZEST FOR 1 MINUTE.

ADD THE BLENDER CONTENTS AND

1 C chicken broth

BRING TO A BOIL, REDUCE HEAT, AND SIMMER, STIRRING OCCASIONALLY, FOR 5 MINUTES.

ADD

2 C white rice
Water, enough to cover the rice by one knuckle, about1.3 cm (1/2 inch)

RAISE THE HEAT AND BOIL UNTIL THE LIQUID IS LEVEL WITH THE RICE. COVER, LOWER HEAT, AND SIMMER 45 MINUTES, OR UNTIL THE LIQUID IS ABSORBED.

STIR GENTLY. ADD AND COMBINE GENTLY.

1 C slivered almonds
1/2 C pistachios, chopped ( or omit the almonds and just use pistachios)
1/2 C fresh parsley, chopped finely (optional)
Salt
Black pepper, ground

This is a good addition to a meal with curry.

## COCONUT RICE

IN A BOWL MIX
2 C coconut milk
1 C raisins
AND SET ASIDE.
TO A FRYING PAN ADD AND HEAT
2 T vegetable oil
ADD
1 onion, finely chopped
FRY UNTIL SOFT.
TURN DOWN HEAT AND ADD
2 C rice, uncooked
MIX THOUROUGHLY.
ADD THE RESERVED COCONUT MIXTURE AND
2 C chicken stock
Salt, to taste
BRING TO A BOIL, LOWER HEAT, AND SIMMER UNTIL THE WATER IS ABSORBED.

## BEEF WITH RICE VERMICELLI

SOAK
250 g (1/2 lb) rice vermicelli, broken up
IN COLD WATER FOR ABOUT 10 MINUTES.
SLICE
500 g (1 lb) lean beef,
INTO 5 cm (2 inch) LENGTHS 6 mm (1/4 inch) THICK.
IN A LARGE POT HEAT
1 T peanut or vegetable oil
ADD
6 C chard, sliced
1 C Chinese snow peas, or sugar peas, or mange tout.
FRY 2 MINUTES ON HIGH, REMOVE FROM POT AND RESERVE.
ADD MORE OIL IF NECESSARY AND ADD
4 garlic cloves, chopped finely
2 tsp ginger, grated
3 T fermented black beans, rinsed and chopped coarsely
FRY, STIRRING, FOR 1 MINUTE. ADD THE BEEF AND COOK UNTIL COLOR CHANGES.
ADD
1 C water
2 T soy sauce
AND THE VERMICELLI. TOSS, COVER, AND SIMMER FOR 5 MINUTES. RETURN VEGETABLES TO POT AND TOSS UNTIL HEATED THROUGH.
SERVE AT ONCE WITH
Chilli oil on the side

This is a convenient way to do lasagna that Kathryn often uses.

## LASAGNE

(180 C (350 F) see times below)
(23 x 30 cm (9x12 inch) greased baking dish)

COOK, BREAKING UP
500 g (1 lb) ground beef
ADD
3 C tomato sauce
1 C water
LADLE HALF OF THE BEEF MIXTURE INTO A BAKING DISH AND COVER WITH A LAYER OF
Lasagna noodles, uncooked
IN A BOWL MIX
2 eggs
2 C cottage cheese
1/2 C parmesan cheese, grated
1 package frozen spinach, thawed and chopped (optional)
POUR OVER THE NOODLE LAYER AND COVER WITH ANOTHER LAYER OF
Lasagna noodles, uncooked
POUR THE REST OF THE TOMATO MIXTURE ON TOP. COVER THE BAKING DISH WITH TINFOIL AND BAKE FOR 45 MINUTES. REMOVE THE TINFOIL AND COVER WITH SLICED, OR GRATED
Mozzarella cheese
BAKE FOR ANOTHER 15 MINUTES UNCOVERED.
MAY BE FROZEN UNCOOKED. REMOVE FROM FREEZER AND THAW BEFORE BAKING AS ABOVE.

# LINGUINI WITH SHRIMP

COOK, DRAIN, AND RESERVE
500 g (1 lb) linguini noodles
IN A POT HEAT
1 T butter
ADD AND FRY
250 g (1/2 lb) fresh shrimp
FOR 1 TO 2 MINUTES AND ADD
1/4 C dry white wine
SIMMER 2 MINUTES AND ADD A MIXTURE OF
1 T corn starch
1 C milk
COOK ON MEDIUM HEAT UNTIL BUBBLING AND SEASON WITH
1/4 tsp salt
1/4 tsp black pepper, ground
ADD THE PASTA TO THE SHRIMP, TOSS, AND HEAT.
GRADUALLY ADD
1/2 C parmesan cheese, coarsely grated
TOSS THOROUGHLY AND HEAT UNTIL CHEESE HAS MELTED.
SPRINKLE WITH
2 tsp fresh parsley, finely chopped
4 tsp parmesan cheese
SERVE.

Another recipe that I always had the pleasure of enjoying when I was a child is this.

## MACARONI AND CHEESE

COOK
500 g (1 lb) elbow macaroni
MIX WITH
500 g (1 lb) ground beef, cooked
1 540 ml (19 oz) Can crushed tomatoes
PUT ALL INTO A CASSEROLE DISH AND TOP WITH
Cheddar cheese, grated
BAKE AT 180 C (350 F) FOR 1 HOUR.

Here is a recipe that ended up being used for something completely different from the original. Much simpler than being used for clams on the half shell.

## CLAM SAUCE FOR PASTA

IN A FRYING PAN HEAT
1T vegetable oil
ADD
1 onion, chopped
FRY UNTIL SOFT AND ADD
5 garlic cloves, chopped finely
FRY UNTIL GARLIC IS JUST COOKED, STIRRING CONSTANTLY, AND ADD
2 400 ml (14 oz) Cans clams, juice reserved
1/4 C clam juice from can
1 T lemon juice
1/4 C fresh parsley, chopped
BRING TO A BOIL, REDUCE HEAT, AND COOK 10 MINUTES. SERVE OVER PASTA.

## TOMATO SAUCE FOR PASTA

IN A POT HEAT

1 T olive oil

1 T butter

ADD AND FRY UNTIL TRANSLUCENT

1 large onion, chopped finely

ADD

1 medium carrot, finely chopped

1 celery stalk, finely chopped

FRY 5 MINUTES AND ADD

2 800 ml (28 oz) Cans tomatoes, finely chopped with liquid

4 T tomato paste

8 garlic cloves, chopped finely

2 tsp dried oregano

1/2 tsp dried basil

1 whole clove, crushed

1 T sugar

1/2 C dry red wine

1 tsp salt

1 tsp black pepper, ground

BRING TO A BOIL, LOWER HEAT, AND SIMMER 1 HOUR.

# VEGETABLES

This has been a staple for pot luck dinners.

## HOMINY IN CHILLI SAUCE

INTO A BOWL PUT

10 garlic cloves, chopped

2 large onions, chopped

6 fresh chillies, sliced thinly in rounds

2 T cilantro (fresh coriander leaves), chopped

1/2 tsp black pepper, ground

Large pinch each of dried marjoram, rosemary, thyme, savory, sage, basil

1/2 tsp cumin powder

3/4 tsp dried oregano

MIX WELL.

HEAT A LARGE POT OR FRYING AND ADD

1/4 C olive oil

ADD THE CONTENTS OF THE BOWL. FRY ON MEDIUM HIGH UNTIL ONIONS BECOME TRANSLUCENT, STIRRING OFTEN. ADD

4 large tomatoes, chopped

1 bay leaf

1 tsp sugar

COOK UNTIL THE SAUCE THICKENS AND ADD

200 ml (6 oz) Can black olives, drained and sliced thinly, reserving 8 whole

1/2 tsp red pepper powder

1 tsp salt

MIX WELL AND STIR IN

1 850 ml (29oz) Can hominy corn, drained and rinsed

COOK UNTIL CORN IS HEATED.

PUT ALL INTO A CASSEROLE DISH AND TOP WITH

1/2 C strong cheddar cheese, grated

1/2 C Swiss cheese, grated

8 olives, thinly sliced

1 T cilantro (fresh coriander leaves), chopped

SERVE.

## CHINESE CABBAGE IN SWEET SOUR HOT SAUCE

HEAT A FRYING PAN, OR WOK AND ADD

3 T vegetable oil
1 T sesame oil
1 tsp red pepper flakes
1 T thick black bean sauce

STIR FRY A FEW SECONDS AND ADD

1 kg (2 lb) Chinese cabbage leaves, cut in 5 cm (2 inch) pieces

STIR FRY VIGOROUSLY UNTIL THE CABBAGE BEGINS TO BECOME LIMP.

IN A SMALL BOWL MIX

2 T soy sauce
2 T vinegar
1 1/2 T sugar
1 tsp salt

ADD TO THE PAN AND COOK 1 MINUTE, STIRRING CONSTANTLY.

ADD

1 T sesame oil

MIX WELL AND SERVE HOT.

## CORN ON THE COB

SHUCK AND REMOVE SILK FROM

Cobs of corn (maize)

IN A LARGE POT BRING TO A BOIL

Water, enough to cover the cobs

PLACE THE COBS IN THE POT AND BRING BACK TO A BOIL. BOIL 8 MINUTES AND REMOVE COBS. SERVE WITH

Butter
Salt

OR WHATEVER YOU PREFER ON YOURS.

## FENNEL a la GRECQUE

TO A POT ADD

2 Fennel Bulbs, separated and large ribs cut in half
1 tsp Salt
Water, enough to cover

BRING TO A BOIL AND COOK 10 MINUTES. DRAIN OFF WATER.

TO THE POT ADD

3/4 C beef broth, or boiling water
3/4 C dry white wine
1/4 C olive oil
2 T lemon juice
6 whole black peppercorns
1 fresh parsley sprig, broken up
1 small bay leaf
1/2 tsp dried basil

COVER AND COOK UNTIL FENNEL IS CRISP-TENDER, ABOUT 5 TO 10 MINUTES. COOL IN LIQUID, OR SERVE HOT.

## CAULIFLOWER WITH CHEESE SAUCE

STEAM AND SET ASIDE

1 cauliflower head, cut up

TO MAKE THE SAUCE MELT IN A SAUCEPAN

2 T butter

AND ADD

2 T all purpose flour

STIR IN AND ADD

1 C milk

WHISK UNTIL IT BOILS, REMOVE FROM HEAT AND ADD

1 C cheddar cheese, grated

STIR UNTIL CHEESE IS MELTED AND WELL INCORPORATED.

## RATATOUILLE

IN A POT HEAT

1 T olive oil

ADD AND FRY UNTIL TRANSLUCENT

1/2 C onion, chopped
4 garlic cloves, chopped

ADD

2 C zucchini, chopped
2 C eggplant, cubed
1/2 tsp dried basil
1/2 tsp dried oregano
2 medium tomatoes, chopped
Pinch black pepper, ground

OPTIONALLY ADD A BOUQUET, TO BE DISCARDED AFTER SIMMERING, OF

Celery leaves
Parsley leaves
1 bay leaf

SIMMER ABOUT 30 MINUTES.

## INDIAN ZUCCHINI

IN A SAUCEPAN HEAT

1 T vegetable oil

ADD

1/2 C onion, chopped

COOK FOR 5 MINUTES WITHOUT BROWNING AND ADD

400 ml (14 oz) Can tomatoes, chopped
2 garlic cloves, crushed
1 inch ginger, grated
1/2 tsp red pepper powder

BRING TO A BOIL AND SIMMER 20 MINUTES, OR UNTIL THICKENED.

ADD AND STIR IN

4 zucchinis, sliced
Salt
Black pepper, ground

COOK 5 MINUTES, STIRRING GENTLY UNTIL ZUCCHINI IS TENDER. REMOVE GINGER PIECES BEFORE SERVING.

Using pablano chillies is not essential here, but I find them to have the best flavor for this recipe. If you don't like the soufle coating, like my son Andrew, proceed with the variation, below.

CHILLIES RELLENOS (stuffed chilli peppers)

CHAR
4 large poblano chillies
UNDER A GRILL UNTIL SKIN BLISTERS, TURNING TO ROAST ALL SIDES. PUT IN A PLASTIC BAG TO SWEAT BEFORE PEELING THE SKIN OFF. MAKE A SLIT DOWN THE LENGTH OF THE PEPPER AND REMOVE THE SEEDS.
STUFF WITH
250 gr (1/2 pound) monterey jack cheese, cut in strips
SEPARATE
3 eggs
AND BEAT THE WHITES UNTIL THEY FORM STIFF PEAKS.
MIX THE EGG YOLKS WITH
1 T milk
1 T vegetable oil
3 T all purpose flour
1/4 tsp salt
UNTIL THICK AND SMOOTH. CAREFULLY FOLD THE YOLK MIXTURE INTO THE EGG WHITES.
DREDGE CHILLIS IN
All purpose flour
PUT HALF THE BATTER IN THE BOTTOM OF A BAKING DISH, PLACE THE STUFFED CHILLIES ON TOP, AND SPREAD THE REMAINING BATTER ON TOP OF THE CHILLIES. BAKE IN A PREHEATED OVEN AT 180 C (350 F) FOR 35 TO 40 MINUTES. SERVE WITH TOMATO SALSA OR GUACAMOLE AND SHREDDED LETTUCE.

VARIATION
DO NOT MAKE EGG SOUFLET OR DREDGE IN FLOUR MIXTURE. BAKE THE STUFFED CHILLIES FOR ABOUT 20 MINUTES OR UNTIL CHEESE IS WELL MELTED.

## INDIAN SWISS CHARD

IN A FRYING PAN HEAT

1 T vegetable oil

ADD

1 T ginger, grated

FRY BRIEFLY AND ADD

1 bunch Swiss chard, cut up

COOK UNTIL WILTED, COVER, AND COOK FOR 6 MINUTES.

ADD, MIXING WELL

2 tsp honey

Dash salt

## GREEK CARROTS

IN A LARGE FRYING PAN HEAT

4 T butter, or margarine

ADD

15 young carrots

FRY UNTIL GOLDEN BROWN AND ADD

4 scallions, finely chopped

3 T fresh parsley, chopped

1/2 tsp dried thyme

1 tsp dried oregano

1/2 tsp sugar

3 T water

1/4 C white wine

1 T butter, or margarine

MIX AND SIMMER, COVERED, FOR 20 MINUTES.

SERVE WITH PAN JUICES POURED OVER.

## CARROTS WITH INDIAN SPICES

PEEL AND SLICE INTO 3mm (1/8 inch) THICK ROUNDS

1.5 kg (3 lb) carrots

SET ASIDE.

IN A SMALL BOWL PUT

1 T fresh ginger, finely chopped

1/4 tsp turmeric powder

SET ASIDE.

IN A LARGE FRYING PAN HEAT

3 T vegetable Oil

ADD

5 fenugreek seeds

1/4 tsp black mustard seeds

WHEN THE SEEDS BEGIN TO POP ADD THE GINGER AND TURMERIC. COOK 2 MINUTES, STIRRING FREQUENTLY AND ADD

1/2 C cilantro (fresh coriander leaves), chopped coarsely

1 fresh green chilli, finely chopped

COOK, STIRRING FREQUENTLY, ANOTHER 3 MINUTES. ADD THE CARROTS AND COOK, STIRRING, 5 MINUTES.

ADD

1 tsp coriander powder

1 tsp cumin powder

1/2 tsp garam masala

1 tsp salt

3 T warm water

STIRR WELL, LOWER HEAT, AND SIMMER 30 MINUTES. STIRR OCASIONALLY.

## HARVARD BEETS

TO A POT ADD AND MIX

1/4 C sugar
1/2 T corn starch

ADD

1/4 C water
1/4 C vinegar

BRING TO A BOIL, TURN OFF HEAT, AND ADD

14 small beets, cubed

LET STAND 30 MINUTES. REHEAT AND ADD

2 T butter

COOK UNTIL BEETS ARE TENDER.

## MARINATED ARTICHOKES

IN A BOWL COMBINE

2 T lemon Juice
2 T olive oil
3 garlic cloves, chopped finely
1 T sugar
1/4 tsp tarragon, (optional)
1 tsp dried oregano
2 T water
6 fresh artichoke hearts, cooked

MARINATE 2 HOURS, OR OVERNIGHT IN THE REFRIGERATOR, BEFORE SERVING.

## EVERLASTING COLE SLAW

INTO A BOWL GRATE

6 C cabbage
4 C carrot
1 C onion

AND RESERVE

INTO A SAUCEPAN ADD AND BRING TO A BOIL

1/2 C vinegar
1/2 C brown sugar
1/2 C vegetable oil
1 tsp salt
1 tsp dry mustard

COOK UNTIL WELL BLENDED.

ADD THIS TO THE VEGETABLES, MIX WELL, AND STORE IN A FRIDGE.

# BREADS AND MUFFINS

I have only done this one once, but it turned out quite good.

## DARK RYE BREAD

(230 C (450 F), 15 minutes, then 180 C (350F) 45 min)

INTO A SMALL POT PUT

1/2 C sugar

AND HEAT TO MEDIUM HIGH. STIR WITH A FORK UNTIL MELTED, SMOKES, AND TURNS BLACK.

ADD

3/4 C boiling water

STIR UNTIL CARAMELIZED SUGAR IS DISSOLVED AND REDUCED TO 1/2 CUP. REMOVE FROM HEAT, SET ASIDE, AND LET COOL.

PEEL AND DICE

2 potatoes

BOIL, DRAIN, MASH, AND SET ASIDE.

DISSOLVE

3 T yeast

IN A MIXTURE OF

2 C warm water

1 tsp sugar

AND LET STAND FOR 10 MINUTES.

MEANWHILE, INTO A BOWL SIFT

6 C rye flour

INTO ANOTHER BOWL PUT

2 C warm water

ADD MASHED POTATOES, YEAST MIXTURE, AND CARAMELIZED SUGAR. ADD THIS MIXTURE TO FLOUR AND BEAT UNTIL SMOOTH.

ADD

1 T salt

1 T caraway seed

6 C rye flour

MIX THOROUGHLY WITH A SPOON. RISE UNTIL DOUBLED. PLACE ON A WELL FLOURED BOARD AND KNEAD IN

3 1/2 to 4 C all purpose flour

UNTIL SMOOTH, BUT NOT QUITE STIFF ENOUGH TO HOLD ITS SHAPE. DIVIDE INTO TWO, SHAPE, AND PLACE EACH ON A FLOURED BAKING SHEET. LET RISE UNTIL DOUBLED. MAKE THREE DIAGONAL SLASHES ON TOP. BAKE AS ABOVE AND REMOVE FROM OVEN. BRUSH TOP WITH COLD WATER AND LET COOL.

## JIMMY'S OATMEAL BREAD

(180 C (350 F) - 60 minutes)

IN A BOWL MIX

1 C rolled oats
1 1/4 C buttermilk

LET STAND 30 MINUTES AND ADD

1/4 C brown sugar
1 egg, beaten
1/4 C vegetable oil

AND BEAT INTO THE OAT MIXTURE.

INTO A BOWL SIFT

1 1/2 C all purpose flour
1 tsp baking powder
1 tsp baking soda
1/2 tsp salt

AND ADD TO THE OAT MIXTURE, MIXING WELL.

PUT ALL INTO A 1.5 L (1 1/2 QUART) GREASED CASSEROLE.

TOP WITH

1/4 C cheddar cheese, grated

BAKE AS ABOVE, COOL 15 MINUTES, AND TURN OUT ONTO A RACK.

## CARROT SESAME SEED BREAD

(180 C (350 F) - 1 hour)

INTO A BOWL PUT

2/3 C raisins

1 C carrots, grated

2/3 C sesame seeds

MIX AND POUR

1 C hot water

OVER THE MIXTURE. STIR AND LET STAND 10 MINUTES.

INTO A LARGE BOWL PUT

1/3 C warm water

INTO THE WATER SPRINKLE

1 1/2 T yeast

STIR AND LET STAND UNTIL FOAMY.

INTO A SMALL BOWL PUT

1 C boiled milk

STIR IN

5 T chopped butter

ADD MILK MIXTURE TO YEAST MIXTURE AND ADD

1/2 C honey

3 C whole wheat flour

BEAT FOR 3 MINUTES AND STIR IN

2 tsp salt

2 1/2 C whole wheat flour

ADD RAISIN MIXTURE AND KNEAD 3 MINUTES ON A FLOURED BOARD. LIGHTLY OIL HANDS AND BOARD. KNEAD 3 MINUTES MORE. COVER AND LET RISE FOR 15 MINUTES. KNEAD LIGHTLY AND PLACE IN AN OILED BOWL UNTIL DOUBLE, 1 1/2 HOURS. DIVIDE IN HALF AND PUT IN PANS. LET THE DOUGH RISE UNTIL DOUBLE, ABOUT 1 HOUR.

BAKE AS ABOVE.

## CRANBERRY BREAD

(180 C (350 F) - 1 hour and 10 minutes)
(23 x 13 x 7.5 cm (9x5x3 inch) greased loaf pan)

INTO A LARGE BOWL SIFT

2 C all purpose flour
1 C sugar
1 1/2 tsp baking powder
1/2 tsp salt
1/2 tsp baking soda

CUT IN

1/4 C butter, or margarine

UNTIL MIXTURE IS CRUMBLY.
ADD THE FOLLOWING MIXTURE, ALL AT ONCE.

1 egg, beaten
1 tsp orange zest
3/4 C orange juice

STIR UNTIL THE DOUGH IS EVENLY MOIST.
FOLD IN

1 1/2 C light raisins
1 1/2 C cranberries, fresh or frozen, chopped

SPOON INTO PAN AND BAKE AS ABOVE.

## BANANA NUT BREAD

(180 C (350 F) - 50 minutes)

IN A BOWL MIX

1 C whole wheat flour
1 C all purpose flour
1/2 C sugar
1/2 C dry milk
1/4 tsp salt
1 C chopped nuts
1/2 C chopped dates, or omit nuts and use 1 C
1 1/2 tsp baking powder

COMBINE IN ANOTHER BOWL

1/4 C vegetable oil
2 eggs
2 C ripe bananas, mashed
1 tsp vanilla extract
1/2 C water
1/2 tsp lemon zest

AND ADD TO FLOUR MIXTURE.

STIR QUICKLY AND POUR INTO LOAF PAN. BAKE AS ABOVE.

## CINNAMON APPLE MUFFINS

(220 C (425 F) - 15-20 minutes)

IN A BOWL COMBINE
2 C  all purpose flour
1/3 C  sugar
1 T  baking powder
1/4 tsp  salt
1 T  cinnamon powder
MIX IN
2  apples, cored and cubed
1 C nuts, chopped
SET ASIDE.
IN ANOTHER BOWL MIX
1  egg, lightly beaten
1/4 C  vegetable oil
2/3 C  apple juice
1 tsp  vanilla extract

ADD WET INGREDIENTS TO DRY AND STIR UNTIL THE BATTER IS JUST MOISTENED AND LUMPY. FILL MUFFIN TINS AND SPRINKLE WITH CINNAMON AND SUGAR.
BAKE AS ABOVE.

## BRAN MUFFINS

(205 C (400 F) – 18 to 20 minutes)

IN A BOWL CREAM

1/4 C shortening
1/4 C brown sugar

ADD

1/4 C molasses
2 eggs

BEAT WELL AND ADD

1 C milk, or 1/2 Cup powdered milk and 1 Cup water
1 1/2 C bran

COMBINE IN ANOTHER BOWL

1 C all purpose flour
1 1/2 tsp baking powder
1/2 tsp baking soda
1/4 tsp salt

ADD TO LIQUID INGREDIENTS AND ADD

1/2 C raisins

MIX AND FILL MUFFIN TINS. BAKE AS ABOVE

VARIATION:

REPLACE SUGAR WITH 1/2 C MOLASSES.
INCREASE BRAN TO 2 C.
REPLACE ALL PURPOSE FLOUR WITH WHOLE WHEAT FLOUR.
REPLACE RAISINS WITH 1 Cup CHOPPED DATES

## CARROT MUFFINS

(190 C (375 F) - 15 minutes)

IN A BOWL MIX

3 C all purpose flour
3 C whole wheat flour
1 T baking soda
3 T baking powder
2 T cinnamon powder
1 tsp salt
4 C bran
1/2 C sugar
1/2 C brown sugar

IN ANOTHER BOWL MIX

2 C vegetable oil
8 eggs
6 C grated carrot
250 g (1/2 lb ) raisins
1/2 C molasses
2 C water

ADD WET INGREDIENTS TO DRY AND PUT IN MUFFIN PANS. BAKE AS ABOVE.

## CHOCOLATE CHIP MUFFINS

(165 C (325 F) - 25 minutes)

INTO A BOWL PUT

1 1/2 C rolled oats

1 C boiling water

3/4 C apple juice

STIR AND LET STAND FOR 20 MINUTES.

COMBINE IN A LARGE BOWL

1 1/2 C all purpose flour

1 1/2 tsp baking powder

1 tsp baking soda

1/2 tsp salt

1 tsp cinnamon powder

1/4 C vegetable oil

1 tsp vanilla extract

SET ASIDE.

TO THE OATS MIXTURE ADD

2 eggs

AND STIR UNTIL SMOOTH.

ADD OATS MIXTURE TO FLOUR MIXTURE AND STIR UNTIL THE DRY INGREDIENTS ARE MOISTENED.

FOLD IN

1/2 C chocolate chips

USE MUFFIN PAN AND BAKE AS ABOVE. MAKES 12 MUFFINS.

## ORANGE-CARROT-COCONUT MUFFINS

(165 C (325F) - 20 minutes)
(greased muffin tins)

SIFT INTO A BOWL

2 C all purpose flour
3/4 C sugar
1 tsp baking soda
2 tsp baking powder
1/4 tsp salt

MIX IN

2 C carrots, grated
1/2 C currants
1/2 C nuts, chopped
1/2 C unsweetened coconut

IN ANOTHER BOWL MIX TOGETHER

Zest of 2 oranges
2 eggs
1/2 C sour cream
1/2 C yogurt
6 T butter, melted
Juice of one orange

ADD WET INGREDIENTS TO DRY AND STIR, DON'T MIX, 14 TO 20 TIMES. SPOON INTO MUFFIN PAN. BAKE AS ABOVE.

# DATE'N OAT MUFFINS

(205 C (400 F) - 20 minutes)
(muffin pan)

COMBINE IN A BOWL AND LET STAND

1 C oats
1 C buttermilk

COMBINE IN ANOTHER BOWL

1 C all purpose flour
1 tsp baking powder
1/2 tsp baking soda
1/2 tsp salt
1/2 tsp cinnamon powder

STIR WELL TO BLEND AND STIR IN

1/3 C brown sugar
1 C chopped dates

ADD THE NEXT TWO INGREDIENTS TO OAT MIXTURE

1 egg, beaten
1/4 C melted butter

MIX WELL

ADD OAT MIXTURE ALL AT ONCE TO BATTER AND STIR UNTIL MOISTENED. PUT IN MUFFIN TINS AND BAKE AS ABOVE. CAN USE BLUEBERRIES, BUT USE 1/2 CUP SUGAR.

## ORANGE MUFFINS

(205 C (400 F) - 15-20 minutes)
(16 muffins)

ADD TO AND BLEND IN A PROCESSOR

Zest of 1 Orange
1 orange, quartered and deseeded
1/3 C orange juice
1/4 C unsalted butter, softened, or 1/4 cup vegetable oil
1 large egg

ADD

1/2 C raisins

BLEND 5 SECONDS AND TRANSFER TO A BOWL.
IN ANOTHER A BOWL SIFT TOGETHER

1 1/2 C all purpose flour
1/3 C sugar
1 tsp baking powder
1 tsp baking soda
1/2 tsp salt

STIR IN ORANGE MIXTURE UNTIL JUST COMBINED.
PUT BATTER IN MUFFIN TINS AND BAKE AS ABOVE.

## VERY BLUEBERRY MUFFINS

(180 C (350 F) - 20-25 minutes)
(makes 12 muffins)

COMBINE IN A BOWL AND SET ASIDE

1 C all purpose flour
1 C whole wheat flour
2 tsp baking powder
1/4 tsp salt

COMBINE IN ANOTHER BOWL

1 C yogurt
1 tsp baking soda

AND SET ASIDE.

TO ANOTHER BOWL ADD

1 egg, beaten
1/4 C water
1 tsp vanilla extract
1/4 C vegetable Oil
1/3 C sugar

STIR WELL AND ADD DRY INGREDIENTS AND YOGURT ALTERNATELY TO LIQUIDS, STIRRING UNTIL JUST COMBINED.

STIR IN

1 C blueberries, or marion berries cut in half, or blackberries

PUT IN MUFFIN PANS AND BAKE AS ABOVE.

## JALAPENO CORNBREAD MUFFINS

(220 C (425F) – 15 to 20 minutes)
(makes 12 muffins)

INTO A BOWL SIFT
1 1/2 C cornmeal
1/2 C all purpose flour
1 T sugar
2 tsp baking powder
1 tsp baking soda
1/4 tsp salt
ADD
1 small onion, chopped finely
MIX AND ADD
1 C cheddar cheese, grated
3 fresh jalapeno chilli peppers, chopped finely
MIX WELL.
IN A SMALL BOWL WHISK TOGETHER
2 eggs
1 1/2 C milk
1 T lemon juice
3 T vegetable oil
ADD WET INGREDIENTS TO DRY AND STIR UNTIL COMBINED WELL. PUT BATTER IN MUFFIN TINS AND BAKE UNTIL LIGHTLY BROWNED.

This is a very sweet waffle, almost a cookie, passed to us from a friend originally from Belgium.

## BELGIAN WAFFLES (Maurice)

IN A BOWL MIX

4 1/2 C all purpose flour
2 C sugar

IN ANOTHER BOWL MIX

500 g (1/2 pound) butter, melted
5 eggs beaten
2 tsp vanilla extract

ADD WET INGREDIENTS TO DRY AND LET SIT AT LEAST 2 HOURS IN FRIDGE. FORM INTO GOLF BALLS. PLACE BALL ON EACH SECTION OF A HOT WAFFLE IRON AND SQUASH IRON SHUT. COOK UNTIL BROWN.

## PANCAKES

MIX

1 1/3 C all purpose flour

3 tsp baking powder

1/4 tsp salt

3 T sugar

MAKE A WELL IN THE FLOUR MIXTURE AND SLOWLY ADD, WHILE MIXING

1 egg, beaten thoroughly

1 1/4 C milk

ADD

3 T butter, melted or vegetable oil

1/4 tsp vanilla extract

STIR QUICKLY UNTIL JUST MIXED AND IS STILL LUMPY.

## BRUCE'S SCONES

(230 C (450 F) - 10 - 12 minutes)

INTO A BOWL PUT

1 3/4 C all purpose flour
4 tsp baking powder
2 T sugar
1/2 tsp salt
1/2 C currants, or raisins

MIX WELL AND CUT IN

1/3 C shortening

COMBINE WELL AND ADD A MIXTURE OF

1 egg, beaten
1/2 C milk

STIR WITH A FORK TO MAKE A STIFF DOUGH. DIVIDE IN HALF. PAT INTO 6 INCH CIRCLES. PLACE ON LIGHTLY GREASED BAKING SHEET. BRUSH WITH MILK AND SPRINKLE WITH

Sugar

SCORE INTO QUARTERS AND BAKE AS ABOVE.

## OAT CAKES

(190 C (375 F) – 10 to 15 minutes)

COMBINE IN A BOWL

1 C whole wheat flour
2 C oatmeal
1 tsp salt
1/2 C fat (best with 1/2 margarine and 1/2 bacon fat)
1/4 C sugar
1/2 tsp baking soda

ADD UP TO

1/3 C water

OR UNTIL POSSIBLE TO ROLL. ROLL STRAIGHT ONTO COOKIE SHEET, FLOURING ROLLING PIN AND HANDS. MARK IN TRIANGLE SHAPES. BAKE AS ABOVE, REMOVE FROM SHEET AND BREAK INTO TRIANGLES.

# CAKES COOKIES AND BARS

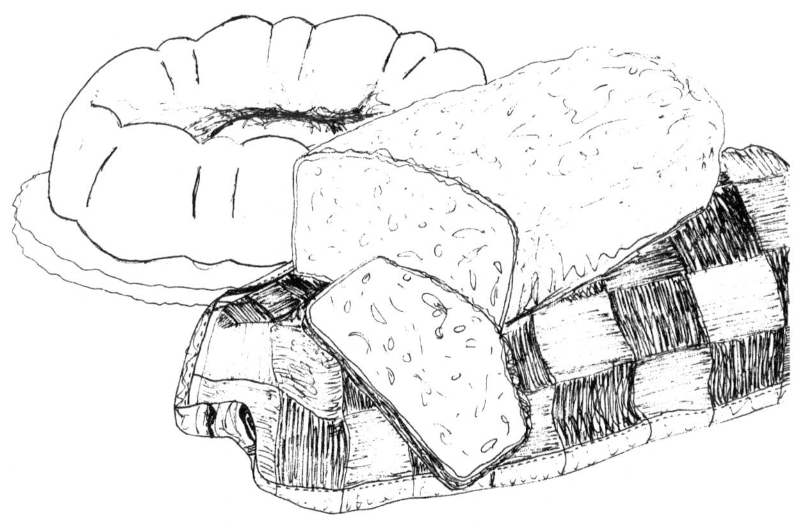

## DAD'S COOKIES

(180 C (350 F) - 10 minutes)

CREAM TOGETHER IN A BOWL

1 C brown sugar
1 C sugar
1 C shortening

ADD

2 eggs

AND BEAT WELL.

MIX IN ANOTHER BOWL

1 C rolled oats
1 C dried coconut flakes
2 C all purpose flour
1 1/2 tsp baking powder
1/2 tsp baking soda
1/2 tsp salt

ADD SUGAR MIXTURE TO DRY INGREDIENTS AND MIX WELL. FORM INTO BALLS AND FLATTEN WITH A WET FORK ONTO A BAKING PAN. BAKE AS ABOVE.

## CHOCOLATE CHIP COOKIES

(180 C (350 F) - 10 minutes)

CREAM IN A BOWL

1/4 C sugar
1/2 C brown sugar
1 egg, beaten
1/2 C shortening

MIX IN ANOTHER BOWL

1 C all purpose flour
1/2 tsp baking powder
1/2 tsp salt
1/2 C nuts
1 C chocolate chips

ADD ALTOGETHER TO CREAMED MIXTURE AND STIR IN

1 tsp vanilla extract

BAKE AS ABOVE.

These are my favorite cookie.

## OLD FASHIONED CHOCOLATE COCONUT OATMEAL COOKIES

(180 C (350 F) – 12 to 15 minutes)

IN A BOWL CREAM THOROUGHLY

1 C butter
1 C sugar
1/2 C brown sugar
1 egg

MIX IN ANOTHER BOWL

1 C all purpose flour
1 C rolled oats
1/4 C wheat germ
3/4 C dried coconut flakes
1 tsp baking powder
1 tsp baking soda

MIX AND ADD TO WET INGREDIENTS. MIX WELL.

STIR IN

1 1/2 C chocolate chips, or raisins

DROP BY TEASPOON FULL ON LIGHTLY GREASED BAKING SHEETS. BAKE AS ABOVE.

VARIATION: (chewy)

REPLACE BUTTER WITH 2/3 CUP MARGARINE. REPLACE WHITE SUGAR WITH 1 CUP BROWN SUGAR. INCREASE EGGS TO TWO. INCREASE OATS TO 1 1/2 CUPS. INCREASE WHEAT GERM TO 1/3 CUP. REDUCE COCONUT TO 1/2 CUP. REDUCE CHOCOLATE CHIPS TO 1 CUP.

## PEANUT BUTTER CHOCOLATE CHIP COOKIES

(180 C (350 F) - 13 minutes)

IN A BOWL MIX

1/2 C butter
1 C peanut butter
1/2 C white sugar
3/4 C brown sugar

ADD

2 eggs
1 tsp vanilla extract

MIX AND ADD A MIXTURE OF

1/4 C water
1 tsp baking soda

MIX AND STIR IN

1 1/2 C all purpose flour
1 1/2 C whole wheat flour

STIR AND ADD

1 C chocolate chips

STIR AND DROP BY THE SPOONFUL ON A COOKIE SHEET AND BAKE AS ABOVE.

## HIGH FIBER COOKIE

(190 C (375 F) - 10 minutes)

IN A BOWL BEAT
1/2 C margarine
ADD AND BEAT IN
1/3 C brown sugar, firmly packed
ADD
1 egg
1/4 C molasses
1/2 tsp vanilla extract
1/2 tsp lemon extract
BEAT WELL AND ADD
1 C rolled oats
IN ANOTHER BOWL MIX TOGETHER
1/4 C whole wheat flour
1/4 C wheat germ
1/4 C soy flour
1/4 C rice polishings
1/2 tsp cinnamon
1 tsp baking soda
Pinch salt
ADD TO FIRST MIXTURE
IN A BLENDER CHOP
1/2 C sunflower seeds
1/4 C soy nuts, unsalted
1/4 C sesame seeds
AND ADD TO DOUGH.
MIX WELL AND ADD
3/4 C raisins
MIX AGAIN AND FORM INTO 1 INCH BALLS AND PLACE ON AN UNGREASED COOKIE SHEET. FLATTEN WITH A FORK AND BAKE AS ABOVE. MAKES 3 DOZEN COOKIES.

## WHITE CAKE

(190 C (375 F) - 35 minutes)

IN A BOWL CREAM
1/2 C  margarine, or butter
1 C  sugar
ADD
2  eggs
1 tsp  vanilla extract
BEAT WELL
MIX IN ANOTHER BOWL
1 3/4 C  all purpose, or cake, flour
3 tsp  baking powder
1/2 tsp  salt
ADD FLOUR MIXTURE TO EGG MIXTURE ALTERNATELY WITH
1 C  milk
PUT IN LAYER PANS AND BAKE AS ABOVE.

## LEMON POPPY-SEED POUND CAKE

(165 C (325 F) - 1 1/4 to 1 1/2 hours)
(greased and floured 23 x 13 cm (9x5 inch) loaf pan)

SIFT TOGETHER INTO A BOWL

2 C all purpose flour
1/2 tsp baking soda
1/4 tsp salt

IN A ANOTHER BOWL COMBINE

3/4 C butter, or margarine, at room temperature
1 1/2 C sugar

AND BEAT UNTIL LIGHT AND FLUFFY.
ADD ONE AT A TIME, BEATING WELL AFTER EACH

3 large eggs, at room temperature

ADD

3 T poppy seeds
1 T lemon zest, grated
1 tsp vanilla extract

BEAT WELL AND ADD FLOUR MIXTURE ALTERNATELY WITH

1 C plain yogurt

THREE ADDITIONS OF THE FLOUR MIXTURE AND TWO OF THE YOGURT MIXTURE. BEAT AT LOW SPEED UNTIL SMOOTH. SPOON BATTER INTO PAN. SHAKE PAN TO LEVEL BATTER AND BAKE AS ABOVE.
REMOVE FROM OVEN AND LET COOL 10 MINUTES BEFORE REMOVING CAKE FROM PAN. SERVE AT ROOM TEMPERATURE.

VARIATION

OMIT SALT. REDUCE BUTTER TO 1/2 CUP. REDUCE SUGAR TO 1 CUP. INCREASE POPPY SEEDS TO 3/8 CUP. REDUCE YOGURT TO 1/2 CUP, AND ADD 1/2 CUP LEMON JUICE.

## SPONGE CAKE FOR STRAWBERRY SHORTCAKE

(325 F for 1 hour, 10 inch tube pan)

IN A BOWL STIR TOGETHER
1 C all purpose flour
Pinch salt
IN ANOTHER BOWL BEAT
6 egg yolks
UNTIL THICK AND PALE IN COLOR
GRADUALLY BEAT IN
1 C sugar
ADD AND STIR IN
1 T lemon juice
1 tsp lemon rind
1 T cold water
FOLD IN DRY INGREDIENTS. SET ASIDE.
IN A BOWL BEAT UNTIL STIFF, BUT NOT DRY
6 egg whites
FOLD WHITES INTO BATTER. PUT IN PAN AND BAKE AS ABOVE UNTIL TOP IS SPRINGY. INVERT PAN ON RACK AND LET CAKE COOL BEFORE REMOVING.

# CHOCOLATE CAKE

(180 C (350 F) - 1 hour)

MIX IN A BOWL

2 C all purpose, or cake, flour
2 C sugar
1/2 tsp salt
2/3 C cocoa powder
1 1/2 tsp baking Soda
3/4 tsp baking Powder

IN ANOTHER BOWL MIX

3 eggs
1 tsp vanilla extract
1 1/4 C milk
3/4 C shortening

ADD WET INGREDIENTS TO DRY INGREDIENTS AND MIX WELL.

BAKE AS ABOVE.

This is the cake my mother often made. It is my favorite simple chocolate cake when topped by a good chocolate icing.

## MOIST CHOCOLATE CAKE

(180 C (350 F) - 40 minutes)
(23 cm x 32 cm ( 9x13 inch) pan)

MIX IN A BOWL

2 C all purpose, or cake, flour
1 1/3 C sugar
1 T baking powder
1/2 tsp salt
6 T cocoa powder

IN ANOTHER BOWL MIX

1 1/3 C milk
1/2 C vegetable oil
1 1/2 tsp vanilla extract
3 eggs, beaten

ADD WET INGREDIENTS TO DRY AND MIX WELL. PUT IN A GREASED PAN AND BAKE AS ABOVE.

## CHOCOLATE MACAROON CAKE

(350 F 40-45 minutes.)

SIFT INTO A BOWL
2 C all purpose flour
1 C sugar
1/2 C cocoa powder
1 T baking powder
1 tsp salt
IN ANOTHER BOWL COMBINE
1 egg beaten
1 1/4 C milk
1/2 C vegetable oil
ADD TO DRY INGREDIENTS; STIR UNTIL JUST MOISTENED. SPREAD HALF THE BATTER IN A GREASED AND COCOA DUSTED 10 INCH TUBE PAN. SPOON THE MACAROON FILLING, (BELOW), IN A RING ON TOP OF THE BATTER. TOP WITH THE REMAINING BATTER. BAKE. COOL IN THE PAN 10 MINUTES. REMOVE AND COOL COMPLETELY.
DRIZZLE WITH VANILLA GLAZE, (BELOW).

MACAROON FILLING
BEAT UNTIL FROTHY
1 egg white
GRADUALLY BEAT IN UNTIL STIFF PEAKS FORM
1/4 C sugar
FOLD IN
1 C dried coconut flakes
1 T all purpose flour

VANILLA GLAZE
COMBINE UNTIL SMOOTH
1 C icing sugar
1 T milk

I prefer this to be made with candied cherries only, as in the variation below. Use red and green cherries for festive color.

## LIGHT CHRISTMAS FRUIT CAKE

(150 C (300 F) - 2 hours)
(two 23x13x8 cm (9x5x3 inch) loaf pans lined with foil)

INTO A BOWL PUT
500 g (1 lb) light raisins, chopped
2 candied pineapple rings, chopped
500 g (1 lb) candied cherries
ADD AND MIX IN
1/2 C all purpose flour
IN ANOTHER BOWL CREAM
1 C margarine
ADD GRADUALLY
1 C sugar
ADD AND BEAT IN
1 tsp vanilla extract
3 eggs, beaten
SIFT INTO ANOTHER BOWL
2 1/2 C all purpose flour
2 tsp baking powder
AND ADD TO THE CREAMED MIXTURE.
STIR IN
400 ml (14 oz) Can crushed pineapple, with juice
MIX WELL AND FOLD IN CANDIED FRUIT.
VARIATION
OMIT RAISINS AND PINEAPPLE AND DOUBLE CHERRIES.

# RHUBARB CAKE

(180 C (350 F) – 40 to 45 minutes)
(32 cm x 23 cm (13x9 inch) greased and floured pan)

IN A LARGE BOWL BEAT
1/4 C sugar
1 1/2 C brown sugar
1/2 C margarine, softened
ADD
1 tsp vanilla extract
1 egg
BEAT WELL.
LIGHTLY SPOON
2 1/2 C all purpose flour
INTO A MEASURING CUP AND LEVEL.
COMBINE FLOUR IN A BOWL WITH
1 tsp baking soda
1/2 tsp salt
ADD DRY INGREDIENTS TO SUGAR MIXTURE ALTERNATELY WITH
1 C buttermilk
BEAT UNTIL WELL COMBINED AND MIX IN
2 C rhubarb, chopped
POUR INTO PAN.
COMBINE
2 T sugar
1/2 tsp cinnamon powder
AND SPRINKLE OVER BATTER IN PAN. BAKE AS ABOVE.

## CARROT CAKE

(180 C (350 F) - 45 minutes)
(bundt pan)

IN A BOWL BEAT

3 eggs
1/2 C brown sugar
1/4 C vegetable oil
1 tsp vanilla extract

MIX IN ANOTHER BOWL

1 C cake flour
1 1/3 C milk powder
1 1/2 C whole wheat flour
1 T baking soda
4 tsp cinnamon powder
3/4 tsp nutmeg, grated
3/4 tsp clove powder

ADD DRY INGREDIENTS TO WET INGREDIENTS AND BEAT.

STIR IN

3 C carrots, grated
1 1/2 C pineapple, crushed
1 C raisins

PUT IN A PAN AND BAKE AS ABOVE.

## CHOCOLATE ZUCCHINI CAKE

(165 C (325 F) - 45 minutes)

IN A BOWL MIX

1 C sugar
2 1/2 C all purpose flour
4 T cocoa powder
1/2 tsp baking powder
1/2 tsp salt
1 tsp baking soda
1/2 tsp cinnamon powder
1/2 tsp clove powder

IN ANOTHER BOWL MIX

1/2 C vegetable oil
2 eggs
1 tsp vanilla extract
1/2 C buttermilk
2 1/2 C zucchini, grated

OPTIONALLY ADD

1 C chocolate chips

ADD WET INGREDIENTS TO DRY AND MIX.
BAKE AS ABOVE.

## BANANA CAKE

(190 C (375 F) - 35 minutes)
(20x30 cm (8x12inch) pan)

INTO A BOWL SIFT

2 C  all purpose flour
3/4 tsp  salt
1 1/2 tsp  baking powder
1 tsp  baking soda
1 1/3 C  sugar

ADD

1/2 C  shortening
1 C  bananas, mashed
1/4 C  sour milk

BEAT 300 TIMES AND ADD

2  eggs
1 tsp  vanilla extract
1/4 C  sour milk

BEAT 180 TIMES.  POUR INTO PAN AND BAKE AS ABOVE.

# DATE LOAF

(180 C (350 F) - 1 hour)
(loaf pan)

INTO A BOWL PUT

1 C dates
1 C raisins
1 tsp baking soda

POUR

1 C boiling water

OVER THE FRUIT. LET STAND UNTIL COOL.
IN ANOTHER BOWL MIX

1 T butter
1 egg
1 C sugar
2 C all purpose flour
1/2 tsp salt

ADD TO THE FRUIT MIXTURE, MIX AND PUT IN PAN.
BAKE AS ABOVE.

Here is an old standard.

## MATRIMONY CAKE

(325 F - 30-35 minutes - 8x14 pan)

MIX TOGETHER LIKE PASTRY

1 1/2 C all purpose flour
1/2 tsp baking soda
1 tsp baking powder
1/4 tsp salt
1 C shortening
1 C brown sugar
1 3/4 C rolled oats

SPREAD HALF OF MIXTURE INTO PAN PRESSING FIRMLY.
COVER WITH THE FOLLOWING DATE MIXTURE.
COMBINE

250 g (1/2 lb) dates, chopped
1/2 C cold water
2 T brown sugar
Zest of 1/2 orange

ADD

2 T orange juice
1 tsp lemon juice

COOK UNTIL SMOOTH. COOL BEFORE SPREADING.
COVER WITH REMAINING PASTRY MIXTURE AND BAKE.

This is more a cake than a bread, but who am I to argue. This one comes from Diana Knowles.

## LEMON BREAD

IN A BOWL CREAM TOGETHER

1/2 C butter

2/3 C sugar

ADD

2 eggs

BEAT WELL AND ADD

Zest of one lemon

2 T lemon juice

1/2 C milk

MIX WELL AND ADD

1 tsp baking powder

1/2 tsp salt

1 1/2 C all purpose flour

MIX WELL, PUT IN A BAKING PAN AND BAKE AT 180 C (350 F) FOR 45 MINUTES. LET COOL AND PRICK ALL OVER WITH A TOOTHPICK.

COVER TOP AND SIDES WITH A MIXTURE OF

1/4 C sugar

1 T lemon juice

LET THE MIXTURE SOAK IN BEFORE SERVING.

## LEMON SQUARES

(180 C (350 F) - 20 minutes)

DOUGH

IN A BOWL MIX

1/2 C margarine, melted

1/2 C brown sugar

SIFT INTO ANOTHER BOWL

3/4 C all purpose flour

1/2 tsp baking powder

1/4 tsp salt

ADD FLOUR MIXTURE TO MARGARINE AND STIR IN

1 1/2 C graham wafer crumbs

FILLING

IN A BOWL MIX

1 Can condensed milk

1/2 C lemon juice

1 tsp lemon zest

PUT 4/5 OF THE DOUGH IN PAN. POUR IN FILLING AND SPRINKLE REMAINDER OF DOUGH ON TOP.
BAKE AS ABOVE.

# NANAIMO BARS

(23 x 30 cm (9x12inch) pan)

IN A BOWL MIX

1/2 C butter, melted
1/4 C sugar
5 T cocoa powder
1 egg
1 tsp vanilla extract
1 C dried coconut
2 C graham wafer crumbs

PRESS INTO PAN.

FOR THE ICEING MIX

2 C icing sugar
1/4 C butter
2 T milk
2 T custard powder

SPREAD ON TOP OF MIXTURE IN PAN.

FOR THE TOPPING MELT

1 T butter
1 square chocolate

POUR OVER ICING AND CHILL.

## PEANUT BUTTER CHOCOLATE BARS

(190 C (375 F) - 15 minutes)
(23x30 cm(9x12 inch) pan)

MIX

6 C instant rolled oats
1 C margarine, melted
3/4 C corn syrup
1 tsp vanilla extract

SPREAD IN PAN, BAKE AS ABOVE, AND COOL.

MELT

1 1/2 C chocolate chips
1 C peanut butter

SPREAD ON TOP OF BAKED BARS AND PLACE PAN IN FRIDGE TO CHILL.

# CHERRY SLICES

(180 C (350 F) - 40 to 50 minutes)
(23x23 cm (9x9 inch) pan)

BASE

IN A BOWL MIX

1 C all purpose flour
2 T icing sugar
1/2 C margarine
salt

PRESS INTO PAN AND BAKE AT 180 C (350 F) 10 MINUTES

TOPPING

MIX

2 eggs, well beaten
1/2 C walnuts, chopped
2 T all purpose flour
1/2 tsp vanilla extract
1/2 tsp almond extract
1 1/2 C brown sugar
1 C maraschino cherries
1/2 C dried coconut flakes
1 tsp baking powder

PUT ON TOP OF MIXTURE IN PAN, BAKE AS ABOVE, AND LET COOL.

ICING

MIX

1/4 C butter
2 T milk
2 T boiling water
6 T icing sugar
Cherry juice

BEAT UNTIL LIKE THICK CREAM AND SPREAD ON TOP.

This is the real thing.

## SCOTTISH SHORTBREAD

(150 C (300 F) - 45 minutes)

IN A BOWL CREAM
500 g (1 lb)  butter
1 1/4 C  berry sugar
ADD, KNEADING IN
4 C  all purpose flour
SHOULD BE 1/2 INCH THICK IN PAN.  BAKE AS ABOVE.

## CHOCOLATE ICING

MIX IN A BOWL
3 T  melted butter
1/4 C  milk
1/2 tsp  vanilla extract
INTO THE MILK MIXTURE SIFT
1/4 C  cocoa powder
2 C  icing sugar
BEAT UNTIL SMOOTH AND FLUFFY.

# DESSERTS AND OTHER GOODIES

## AMBROSIA

MIX

500 ml (2 C) sour cream
1 1/2 C sweet dried coconut flakes
1 bag mini marshmallows
500 ml (19 oz) Can pineapple, drained
200 ml (10 oz) Can mandarin oranges, drained

## APPLE CRISP

(180 C (350 F) – 35 to 40 minutes)
(greased baking dish)

IN A BOWL MIX

1 C all purpose flour
1 C rolled oats
1 C brown sugar
1 tsp cinnamon powder
1/2 C margarine

MIX 1/4 OF THE ABOVE WITH

4 C apples, sliced

SPREAD APPLES IN PAN AND TOP WITH REST OF MIXTURE.
BAKE AS ABOVE.

## SURREY SUMMER TRIFLE

IN A SAUCEPAN COMBINE

3 C raspberries (fresh or frozen)

1 C red currants

1/2 C sugar

STIR OVER LOW HEAT TO DISSOLVE SUGAR AND SIMMER 5 MINUTES. REMOVE FROM HEAT AND ALLOW TO COOL.

IN A SERVING BOWL ARRANGE

4 sponge cake shells, split in half

AND COVER WITH THE ABOVE FRUIT AND JUICES.

CUSTARD

IN A BOWL BEAT

6 egg yolks

ADD

1/4 C sugar

2 tsp cornstarch

WHISK THOROUGHLY TO BLEND.

IN A SAUCEPAN HEAT SLOWLY TO A SIMMER

2 C heavy cream

POUR THE CREAM INTO THE EGG MIXTURE, A LITTLE AT A TIME, BLENDING WELL. STRAIN BACK INTO THE SAUCEPAN AND STIR OVER LOW HEAT UNTIL THICKENED, ( DO NOT BOIL).

ADD AND MIX IN

1 tsp vanilla extract

AND COOL SLIGHTLY. POUR CUSTARD OVER FRUIT.

COOL AND CHILL UNTIL FIRM.

JUST BEFORE SERVING SPRINKLE WITH

Almond flakes, toasted

## LAZY DAISY DUFF

(180 C (350 F) - 35 minutes)
(20 cm (8 inch) square pan)

IN THE PAN MELT
1/4 C butter
AND SET ASIDE.
IN A SMALL BOWL MIX
1 C all purpose flour
1/2 C sugar
1 T baking powder
1 pinch salt
QUICKLY STIR IN
2/3 C milk
SPOON THE BATTER OVER THE MELTED BUTTER.
TOP WITH BUT DO NOT STIR IN
2 C chopped fruit, (berries are best)
BAKE AS ABOVE.

This would often be dessert when apples were in season when I was young.

## GRATED APPLES

PEEL, CORE, AND GRATE INTO A BOWL FOR EACH PERSON
Apples
SPRINKLE WITH
Sugar
LET SIT A FEW MINUTES, WHICH ALOWS SOME OXIDATION, ADDING TO THE FLAVOR. MIX AND SERVE. THIS IS A VERY SIMPLE AND DELICIOUS DESSERT.

This is an old standard British recipe passed on by Diana Knowles.

## TRADITIONAL ENGLISH PLUM PUDDING

IN A LARGE BOWL MIX

250 g (1/2 lb) suet (preferably fresh)
2 C raisins
2 C currants
250 g (1/2 lb) mixed peel
2 1/2 C bread crumbs
5 1/2 heaped tablespoons all purpose flour
1 C sugar
2 apples, chopped finely
1 tsp nutmeg, grated
1 tsp ginger
1/2 tsp salt
4 Eggs
1/3 C brandy, or whisky
2 tsp lemon juice
Milk, to make it moist

BOIL IN A CLOTH BAG 7 TO 8 HOURS.
TO SERVE POUR

1/2 C brandy, warmed

OVER THE PUDDING AND FLAMBÉ.
SERVE WITH BRANDY HARD SAUCE.

## BRANDY HARD SAUCE

BEAT UNTIL CREAMY

6 T unsalted butter

ADD, A LITTLE AT A TIME, BEATING UNTIL WHITE AND FLUFFY

1 C icing sugar

ADD, GRADUALLY, BEATING CONSTANTLY

1T brandy, or other liquor

## APPLE CINNAMON BREAD PUDING

(180 C (350 F) - 1 hour)

IN A BOWL THOUROUGHLY MIX

1 1/2 C milk

3 eggs

2 T sugar

1 T vegetable oil

1 tsp cinnamon powder

1/2 tsp vanilla extract

1/4 tsp nutmeg, grated

1/4 tsp salt

ADD

3 slices white bread, cubed and dried

3 apples, chopped

MIX WELL. PUT MIXTURE IN A OILED CASSEROLE DISH AND PLACE DISH IN A BAKING PAN TO WHICH HAS BEEN ADDED

1/2 inch water

BAKE AS ABOVE.

## RICE AND RAISIN PUDDING

INTO A POT PUT

1/2 C uncooked rice

1 C water

BRING TO A BOIL, REDUCE HEAT AND SIMMER UNTIL WATER IS ABSORBED.

CONTINUE COOKING ADDING

1 1/2 C milk

1/2 tsp salt

1/2 C sugar

MIX AND CONTINUE COOKING UNTIL LIQUID IS ABSORBED.

ADD

1 egg, beaten

MIX AND COOK 2 MINUTES.

ADD AND MIX IN

1/3 C raisins

REMOVE FROM HEAT.

# RHUBARB KUCHEN

(180 C (350 F) – 45 to 50 minutes)
(25 cm (10 inch) oiled springform pan)

IN A BOWL CREAM
3/4 C butter
3/4 C sugar
AND BEAT IN
1/3 C plain yogurt
1 egg yolk
1 tsp orange zest
COMBINE IN ANOTHER BOWL
2 C all purpose flour
1/2 tsp baking soda
1 pinch salt
1/2 C almonds, sliced
GRADUALLY STIR INTO THE BUTTER MIXTURE UNTIL INCORPORATED. SPREAD DOUGH EVENLY ONTO BOTTOM, AND (2 CM) 3/4 INCH UP THE SIDES, OF THE SPRINGFORM PAN.
IN A BOWL TOSS
5 C rhubarb, cut in (2.5 cm) 1 inch pieces
1/2 C sugar
1 T orange juice
ARRANGE EVENLY OVER THE DOUGH AND SPRINKLE EDGE WITH
1/2 C almonds
BAKE AS ABOVE UNTIL PASTRY EDGE IS GOLDEN BROWN, AND THE RHUBARB IS TENDER. LET COOL ON RACK.
TO MAKE A GLAZE, BRING TO A BOIL
1/3 C strawberry jelly
3 T water
LOWER HEAT AND BOIL ABOUT 3 MINUTES. BRUSH OVER RHUBARB AND SIDES OF CAKE. LET STAND 5 MINUTES.

## PUMPKIN PIE

(230 C (450 F) - 10 minutes, and then 165 C (325 F) - 35 minutes)

IN A BOWL MIX TOGETHER

2 T all purpose flour
1/2 tsp salt
1/2 tsp fresh ginger, grated
1/2 tsp mace, grated
1/2 tsp nutmeg, grated
1/2 tsp cinnamon powder
1/3 C brown sugar
1/4 C maple syrup
1 C scalded milk
2 eggs, well beaten
1 1/2 C canned pumpkin

POUR MIXTURE INTO A

25 cm (10 inch) unbaked pie shell

BAKE AS ABOVE, OR UNTIL AN INSERTE KNIFE COMES OUT CLEAN.

## IMPOSSIBLE PIE

(180 C (350 F) - 1 hour)
(10 inch pie pan)

IN A BOWL BEAT TOGETHER

4 eggs
1/2 C margarine
2 C milk
1/2 C all purpose flour
1 C dried coconut flakes
2 tsp vanilla extract
1 C sugar

BAKE AS ABOVE. FORMS CRUST, FILLING AND TOPPING ITSELF.

## PINEAPPLE CHEESE CAKE

IN A BOWL BEAT TOGETHER

250 g (8 oz) cream cheese
1/4 C icing sugar, sifted

UNTIL SOFT AND CREAMY.

FOLD IN

2 C whipping cream, beaten until quite stiff
Crushed pineapple (optional)

PLACE IN A COOL

Graham wafer crust (Recipe follows)

CHILL AND TOP WITH FRUIT PRESERVES.

VARIATION

IF BERRIES ARE PUT ON TOP AND THERE IS NO PINEAPPLE USE 1/2 CUP ICING SUGAR.

## GRAHAM WAFER CRUST

(165 C (325F) - 10 minutes)

IN A BOWL MIX

1 1/2 C graham wafer crumbs
1tsp all purpose flour
1/4 C butter, melted
2 tsp sugar

SPREAD OVER BOTTOM AND SIDES OF A PIE PAN AND.
BAKE AS ABOVE

## RAISIN PIE

(230 C (450 F) - 10 minutes), or
(180 C (350 F) - 30 minutes)

IN A BOWL COMBINE

2 C seeded muscat raisins
2 C cold water
2 T lemon juice, or cider vinegar
2 T corn starch
3/4 C sugar
2 T margarine
1/2 tsp cinnamon powder

BRING TO A BOIL AND BOIL 2 MINUTES.
INTO A PIE PAN PLACE

1 pie shell

POUR THE PIE FILLING INO THE SHELL AND BAKE AS ABOVE.

## ELLEN'S RUM BALLS

IN A SAUCPAN MELT
250 g (1/2 lb) margarine
REMOVE FROM HEAT AND ADD
3 C oatmeal
4 T cocoa powder
1 C icing sugar
Milk
1/4 C rum, or brandy
1/2 tsp almond extract
MIX UNTIL SOFT AND WORKABLE
FORM INTO 2.5 cm (1 INCH) BALLS AND ROLL IN
Dried coconut flakes
REFRIGERATE.

## SUPER CHOCOLATE FUDGE

IN A HEAVY SAUCEPAN, OVER LOW HEAT MELT
350 g (3/4 lb) semi sweet chocolate chips,
1 Can sweetened condensed milk
STIR IN
1 1/4 C icing sugar
1 tsp vanilla extract
1/2 C nuts, chopped
Pinch salt
SPREAD EVENLY OVER WAXED PAPER IN A 20 cm (8 INCH) SQUARE PAN. CHILL 3 HOURS. TURN OUT AND REMOVE PAPER.

## CHINESE WALNUTS

IN A LARGE POT BRING

6 C water

TO A BOIL AND ADD

4 C California walnuts

BRING BACK TO A BOIL AND COOK ONE MINUTE.
RINSE WALNUTS UNDER HOT WATER AND DRAIN.
PUT WALNUTS IN A BOWL AND ADD

1/2 C sugar

MIX WELL UNTIL SUGAR MELTS.
WASH POT AND DRY WELL. IN THE POT HEAT

2.3 cm (1 inch) vegetable oil

TO 180 C (350 F). ADD WALNUTS AND FRY 5 MINUTES, OR UNTIL GOLDEN. DRAIN IN SYVE AND SPRINKLE WITH

Salt

PUT ON PAPER TOWELS FOR A FEW MINUTES.

## FRUIT DIP

CREAM IN A BOWL UNTIL FLUFFY

125 g (4 oz) cream cheese

GRADUALLY ADD

3 T milk

ADD, BEATING CONSTANTLY

2 T honey
1 T lemon juice
1 tsp lemon zest

IN ANOTHER BOWL WHIP

1 1/2 C whipping cream

FOLD INTO CHEESE MIXTURE AND CHILL.

## *C*

***D***

*E*



*F*



*G*

### H



### I



### J



### K



### L

***M***



***N***



***O***

## *P*

## *T*

## *V*



## *W*



## *Y*



## *Z*

www.ingramcontent.com/pod-product-compliance
Ingram Content Group UK Ltd.
Pitfield, Milton Keynes, MK11 3LW, UK
UKHW020144250726
13967UKWH00002B/863

9 781425 162658